THE
'OBSCURISM'
OF
LIGHT

A Theological Study into
the Nature of Light

IAIN M. MacKENZIE
Canon Residentiary of Worcester

with a Translation of
Robert Grosseteste's *De Luce* by Julian Lock

The Canterbury Press
Norwich

First published 1996 by The Canterbury Press Norwich
(a publishing imprint of Hymns Ancient & Modern Limited
a registered charity)
St Mary's Works, St Mary's Plain,
Norwich, Norfolk, NR3 3BH

British Library Cataloguing in Publication Data

A catalogue record for this book is available
from the British Library

ISBN 1–85311–147–3

*Typeset by David Gregson Associates
Beccles, Suffolk
Printed in Great Britain by
Athenæum Press Ltd., Tyne & Wear*

BY THE SAME AUTHOR

The Dynamism of Space (1995)
The Anachronism of Time (1994)

For
Neville and Helen Bennett and
Bernard and Barbara Hooper
with all love and gratitude

Contents

CONTENTS

Foreword

It is no matter of form to say that I am honoured to write the foreword to this, the third book in a trilogy by Canon Iain MacKenzie. The first two, *The Anachronism of Time* and *The Dynamism of Space* were commended by academics, Professor Tom Torrance and Bishop David Jenkins. This the third, *The 'Obscurism' of Light*, is commended by me, Iain MacKenzie's own bishop and, I am pleased to say, his friend.

It enables me to pay tribute to the determination of Iain MacKenzie to be a scholarly residentiary canon. Worcester Cathedral, like other cathedrals, has the usual and honoured daily round of prayer and worship as well as a full programme of many other activities, not to mention pastoral demands. Add to these things the computerisation of the six thousand volumes of ancient books in the Cathedral Library, conservation work on many manuscripts, particularly the *Liber Albus*, and you may wonder when the writing of books can be done. It has no doubt been effected by early rising and late nights.

Iain MacKenzie has a prodigious knowledge of the Fathers and of medieval Scholasticism. He moves with ease in their world. The reading of this book is a challenge to those of us who are children of the scientific revolution. For us to understand a thing is immediately to analyse. However, there is also a time to synthesise, to reflect upon things as they present themselves to us in their wholeness. Certainly theology was born into the world as an attempt to reflect upon God in Himself simply. The result may show us much of what we cannot know, but it is a legitimate, no necessary, exercise. It is the prerequisite of prayer and the consort of adoration.

So Iain MacKenzie asks us to contemplate light in its 'instantaneous and omnidirectional diffusion', so near to that uncreated light which is God Himself. It is also to be compared to that light in the human mind, 'the light that enlightens everyman', every intelligent and sentient being, thereby effecting both the diversity and the unity of the creation.

I can only hope that those who wish to draw from the Fathers, from the Scholastics, including Grosseteste and above all Anselm, will read this book. They will find themselves contemplating God and His incarnation in Christ. I have not done it justice. You must persevere with Iain MacKenzie.

+Philip Worcester

Acknowledgements

I should mention, straightaway, that the word 'Obscurism' in the title of this book does not appear in any dictionary. I have taken the view that even if it does not exist, there should be such a word. It is meant to convey the tantalising mystery of light, which, by its very nature, always takes precedence over our thoughts and is elusive of our attempts to analyse it. I trust that no reviewer will equate it with 'obscurantism', and realize that I make myself a hostage to fortune in so mentioning this.

As with the first two books in this trilogy, *The Anarchonism of Time* and *The Dynamism of Space*, the present work is written more in the mode of encouraging others to take up the theme, than in producing conclusions. Indeed the very nature of the themes of time, space and light, inconclusive as they are in the realms of scientific endeavour within the observable universe, can hardly be expected to merit a theological enquiry which is conclusive, dealing as it must not only with creation but with the nature of the Creator. This work, therefore, is to be regarded as a pointer and an encouragement to further enquiry, and I trust that it will be read in this light.

The Bishop of Worcester kindly agreed to write the Foreword, and I wish to take the opportunity to thank him not only for this, but also for all the kindness I have experienced from him, as Diocesan, in many ways in his patronage of theological endeavour.

The text includes a translation by Julian Lock, formerly of Magdalen College, Oxford, of Robert Grosseteste's *De Luce*. The only Latin text of this work conveniently available to us was L. Baur's edition which is somewhat questionable in parts. However, the substance of Grosseteste's thesis is there, and it is hoped that this translation will make this important 13th century work, full as it is with insights into the nature of light before its time, more generally available than any of the out of print translations. I am grateful to Dr Lock for the time and care he has expended on undertaking this translation.

I am also grateful to Mr Giles Gasper of Christ Church, Oxford, for the valuable help he has been in making certain suggestions from the discipline of History, particularly concerning St Anselm. To Mrs Winifred Young of the Cathedral congregation in Worcester I am indebted for proof reading and for encouragement in the production of all three books.

My wife and children have again been encouraging and understanding when some of the material in this book has been put together, of necessity, in holiday time, and they have given me every support possible throughout its writing. My thirteen year old son, Rorie, inventively produced the cover for the book, and I am greatly obliged to him for so doing.

To Mr Kenneth Baker and the Staff of The Canterbury Press Norwich, I again owe much. They have shown unfailing courtesy and assistance in all stages of the publishing of this trilogy, and it is with pleasure that I acknowledge and record this here again.

The use of the words 'man' and 'mankind' in the text is generic in keeping with the original texts, and is not to be construed as exclusive.

For permissions to quote, I am obliged to the following:

The British Academy for the various references to Grosseteste's Hexaemeron;

The Clarendon Press for quotations from J. McEvoy: The Philosophy of Robert Grosseteste, and R. Southern: Robert Grosseteste: The Growth of an English Mind in Medieval Europe. T. and T. Clark, Edinburgh, for excerpts from Karl Barth, Church Dogmatics; T. F. Torrance for references to those of his works formerly published by Christian Journals, Belfast. The Cambridge University Press, the Crown's Patentee, for extracts from the Authorised Version of the Bible (the King James Bible), the rights in which are vested in the Crown.

I.M.M.

Prologue

IN BOTH theology and natural science, light holds a central and determinative role for the nature and pursuit of their respective disciplines as they speak out to the realities of the created dimension and seek to penetrate the verities of the created order. Nowhere is this more obvious than in the place accorded to light in all the development and achievement of post-Einsteinian thought.

The very nature of theology (even if it has more often than not disregarded its own integrity) demands that a consideration of light hold a foremost place in its deliberations; for the God of whom it speaks is the One who is himself uncreated Light, *dwelling in light unapproachable*.[1] Throughout the development of theology several names stand out of persons who took the question of the nature of light and its significance seriously, and made contributions to the understanding of creation in relation to the Creator – some of these achievements being lasting and recognizable, some requiring to be rediscovered, reclaimed out of the forgetfulness or the dismissal of later ages, and repeated for the benefit of our own.

This fundamental importance of light centres on the rationality both of the creation itself and the processes of the mind. This has not always been realized, or sometimes has been overshadowed by other contrived systems of knowledge to the detriment of the integrity of theology. Yet the unfolding of the epic of human thought demonstrates that, from time to time, certain figures have perceived the importance and necessary place of light in such undertakings, and in so doing have enlarged the boundaries of perception and understanding of this universe in the midst of which we live, move and have our being as an integral and significant part of it.

Light is that unifying factor, not only of the fields of being and their relativities within creation, but of the totality of all creation in its essential relation to the Creator who brought

1

it into being and sustains it. It is also that illuminating factor whereby the mind is enlightened and thereby enabled to perceive and appreciate this unity and relation as the inherent clarification of all existence.

That God is uncreated Life and Light, utterly beyond and surpassing our comprehension, yet the Source of all light both enlightening and enlivening, and that our created light and life is grounded in that uncreated Life and Light as is declared and fulfilled in the incarnation, is (or ought to be) the foundation and controlling tenet of that which claims to be the discipline of theology.

Light is, as Robert Grosseteste noted in the 13th century[2] (and the 6th century Alexandrian thinker, John Philoponos, well before him), the most refined form of matter. Its speed and its behaviour is constant, and in this constancy lies the rationality and order and comprehensibility of the universe. The whole cosmos is ordered and harmonized throughout in accord with the principle of the primacy of light.

Light is fundamental and, in the strict sense of the word, primordial, in that it needs no prior created medium for its transmission. It transmits itself, for it depends on no other created agency to realize or even assist that action. Light is autonomous, and on that autonomy rests the natural law of all existence. It is the first movement within creation, and on that motion all life depends. It is, again as Grosseteste emphasized, the prime and superior created entity. Creation is typified as a creation of rationality, for it is a creation of the order of light.

But, as theology has emphasized from time to time, this created light as the ground and constituent meaning of all things, can only be understood in the context of that which, in turn, gives it ground and meaning – the uncreated Light which God is. This uncreated Light is not part of a sequence of supposed infinite dependencies, for it is that which is the source of all, and which admits no superior. It is qualitatively different from creation, yet is the author of all things made. Creation has its bounds. It is finite. Beyond that there is only the Infinity of God which is not finitude writ large or endlessly, but which is utterly other than that which is finite. The quantity of creation, and therefore any quantitative approach to its realities, stops short at the difference between the quality of creation and the quality of God. There is nothing 'beyond' creation in a spatial sense, only in a qualitative one. It is in its relation to this ultimacy of God that light is to be understood; otherwise all our perception, grasp and understanding of all created entities and their relation one to another and to all, would be meaningless, as the light which characterizes their existence would itself be devoid of ultimate meaning, for it would be without ultimate reference.

The incarnation is in itself this relation of created light to uncreated Light. For here, the Light of Light, the Word one with the Father and the Spirit, takes our creaturely frame and nature into union with himself without compromise, diminution or change of the divine nature or the human nature. The Word by whom all things are made gives existence to the human nature which he assumes within his divine existence, and is thereby the Word made flesh, Jesus Christ.

The unapproachable, incomprehensible and invisible Light which God is, has approached us and revealed himself to us, enlightening us without overwhelming, extinguishing or replacing our existence of created light by the utter Otherness of his uncreated Light, but rather grounding it in its Source and affirming it in its integrity as contingent to and from God.

The incarnation is the fact, event and Person of the Word by whom all things are made entering, and taking to himself, our created realities. In the context of the incarnation, any consideration of light is seen to be a threefold consideration: the created light on which nature depends as the ground of its intelligibility and existence; the light of intelligibility which enlightens and informs the mind and which is closely related to physical light; and the uncreated Light which is God himself who, by created light, has bestowed on creation a rationality which corresponds in its created dimension to the uncreated Rationality which he is as uncreated Light.

The cardinal and totally related themes of incarnation, light and life, are held together in theological consideration. They are not to be separated, and, if this study emphasises the subject of light, it does so and undertakes its aim in the knowledge of that necessary relation. It will also underline the relation of created light to uncreated Light, and in so doing involve a consideration of the relation of creation to Creator as one of double contingency. That is to say, that the creation is perceived as dependent upon God for its beginning, its order and upholding, and its fulfilment, and therefore contingent *to* God, but that has bestowed upon it its own dimension, nature and identity as a created identity other than God, and therefore contingent *from* God.

If this study dwells much on the achievements of Robert Grosseteste (c.1170-1253), it does so by way of instancing him as an example of those theologians who, through the ages, have grasped and considered the significance of light and the need of theology to accord it due place in its expression and practice. He is an instance of a thinker who achieved a radical breakthrough on the subject of light, and whose insight has spanned the ages to the extent that his thought processes would raise a feeling of familiar accord, I am sure, amongst some in the world of post-Einsteinian natural science. Indeed, it is tempting to muse (though historical speculation is to be shunned, for it can never make a case and the verdict can never be anything but 'not proven') that had there been a progress such as an unhampered and evenly-coursed evolution on the matter of light after the manner and achievement of Grosseteste on the subject, our present understanding of the universe and the great truths now unfolding in both macroscopic and microscopic dimensions of its realities, in the immensities of space and in the intensities of the smallest particles of matter, might have unfolded much earlier. But it belongs neither to the process of the evolution of species nor to the development of human thought to progress on such untroubled and uninterrupted lines. Too much of human achievement and insight, so hardly won, has been overcome and suppressed by other considerations.

The far-reaching insight of the Nicene Fathers, for example, became tied and mis-shaped by the onrush of that later scholasticism which owed its main thrust to Aristotelian concepts. The perception of God as the Unmoved Mover was resurrected through figures such as Peter Lombard (c. 1100-1160), whose influence perhaps best epitomized by his

dictum *God does not become anything*, had such questionable and lasting effects on the understanding of the relation
of creation to Creator, particularly when taken up by that
theology which took its colour from Thomas Aquinas. This
is not in any way to dismiss Aquinas *in toto*. Far from it. But
his particular employment of Aristotelianism did implant the
acceptance of static concepts and categories into mediaeval
theology as opposed to the flow encouraged by Grosseteste
and Duns Scotus.

The genius of Grosseteste with its remarkable insight into
light and the corresponding idea of the double contingency
of creation, was swamped by the more ecclesiastically, polit-
ically correct and backed Thomist outlook. To criticize
Aquinas ('who after all was canonized') and prefer Grosseteste ('who was not canonized', or even just 'who?') is a
dangerous business, and is but one example of the difficulty
of contradicting the common habit of accepting of personages interpreted merely by historical standing rather than by
the theological criticism of the content of their works. But
such tasks ought to be undertaken even when, or especially
when, the general perception of persons and their significance in the development of thought has become dulled with
repetition, so that the mythology of their value has become
the accepted norm of judgement.

In this study it is hoped to establish the importance of the
concept of light, to offer a more profound appreciation of
some of those who have engaged with it, and to point to their
efforts as fertile and fruitful times in the endeavour of human
thought as it sought a deeper understanding of the relation
between creature and Creator, and therefore of the dignity,
office and estate of the rationality of humanity at the heart of
God's handiwork, with all the awe and reverence which that
universe in all the intricacy of its structured relations where
even chaos is the servant of order, should call forth.

1

Light: the first of all creation

ACCORDING to Basil that which has a beginning has, inevitably, an end[1]:

> If there has been a beginning, do not doubt the end.

In this principle he was preceded by Aristotle in *De Caelo et Mundi*, though not as applied precisely here. Basil warns in this section of his *Hexaemeron* against the misconceived way of thinking which, observing the circular movement of the heavenly bodies, fallaciously concludes the fact that, because we cannot observe where a circle begins and where it ends, therefore these bodies are by nature without a beginning and an end. Such mathematical inferences are, in Basil's view, *laborious vanity*. He emphasises at great length the import of the word *beginning* in Genesis I:1, the thrust of which is that only God has no beginning and end and that creation, having beginning and end as its qualitatively different nature and identity to God, is thus seen to be utterly dependent upon God for its existence, its continuance and its fulfilment.

The creation narrative of Genesis which begins at the first verse of the first chapter may have its conclusion in the first verse of the second chapter: *Thus the heavens and the earth were finished,* and in the fourth verse: *These are the generations of the heaven and of the earth when they were created, and in the day that the Lord God made the earth and the heavens.* The section bounded by these verses may well be taken as a postscript, a concluding statement, summing up all that has gone before in the account of the unfolding of the creative act of God. Verses two and three make mention of the seventh day of creation, a day unlike the preceding six, in that it has no morning or evening. It is the time of creation as it is in its completion.

But the word *generation* does not refer to any idea that the

7

creation is eternally self-generating or self-sustaining. Elsewhere and throughout Genesis, its application refers to the beginning and end of the history of certain personages and people. Its usage is in a different category from that of the myths of the ancient near east which the whole biblical epic of creation approximates, but to the general tenor of which it is at variance in its particular usage of terminology. The use of *generations* is qualified by *the beginning*. There is no such term as the latter in its decisive and uncompromising use here, in the corresponding and surrounding myths in the cultures of the ancient near east. *Beginning* is the absolute and uncompromising determinative of all that follows. *Generations* is the totality of God's handiwork.

However, verse 2 may still raise a question, for it would seem to be positing if not a parallel at least a similar idea to that found in these surrounding myths of the contemporary ancient near east. This is instanced by what might seem to be suggested by

> The earth was without form and void; and darkness was upon the face of the deep.

The Septuagint has αρατος και ακατασκευαστος (*invisible or unseen, and unwrought or unformed or chaotic*) for *without form and void*, though the term αβυσσος, *the gulf, the void,* is also introduced. The various Latin versions render the phrase *invisibilis et incomposita*, following αορατος, or *informis et inanis*, or *inanis et vacuo* (Jerome), which latter two are closer to the Hebrew *tohu wa-bohu, without form and void*. Basil emphasises the concept of invisibility in his exegesis involving an explanation as to why the earth should be invisible. To some extent the rendering *invisible* cloaks the issue, though it is not without a particular and positive slant on the richness of possible interpretations.

What is at stake is set out by Augustine in *Confessions XII:21* where he lists five interpretations of the phrase *tohu wa-bohu*. 1. Does it refer to the supposed stuff of bodily and earthly things, created by God at this point without form, order or light? 2. Does it refer to that, again without form, order or light, from which the sensible heaven and earth, with all the entities involved in both, were to be created?

3. Does it refer to that self-same formless, chaotic and non-enlightened material out of which the higher heaven, as well as the observable heaven and the earth were to be made? 4. Does it refer to a pre-existent material out of which the totality of creation was achieved? 5. Does it refer to a pre-existent material out of which the earth was created?

Out of these questions, two background issues arise. First, as suggested by the last two interpretations noted by Augustine, there is a general two-fold dilemma. Is there any suggestion at all in this verse that there was such a material in chaotic condition pre-existing creation, and thus a primaeval *tertium quid*, something existing independently apart from God and creation? Or, is there the suggestion that creation begins with the bringing into being of a substance without form, order or light? Accepting uncritically for the time being the usage of the idea of 'formlessness' or 'chaos', this dilemma may be resolved into a more basic question, namely: Is creation construed in Genesis in terms of a *creatio ex nihilo*, or is creation seen as an act of God merely bringing order out of pre-existing chaos? Is it truly creation, or a manipulation on the part of God?

No doubt a parallel can be drawn between the Genesis account of creation and the Babylonian epic of creation, known after the first words of its text as *Enuma Elis*[2], in which the god Marduk subdues the chaos monster Tiamat, and creates the visible world by splitting her body into two parts, the one forming the arch of heaven.

Augustine is quite clear that nothing can exist in any sense parallel to, or commensurate with, the eternal being of God. All that is not God is created. He alone is the Uncreate. Whatever may be implied by the phrase *without form and void*, it is not to be interpreted as some sort of eternal matter out of which God created the substance of the heaven and the earth. It has a beginning; God has not.

Karl Barth is uncompromising in his interpretation of the phrase[3]. He gathers together the various historical comments as to its meaning, but is categorical in his assertion that it means not some 'thing', not even darkness in the sense that darkness exists by itself, but that which God rejects as any possibility concerning what his creation is to be. A rudimentary state of formlessness is rejected. It has no reality for it is that which contradicts reality. It is the impossible alternative to reality; it threatens creation in that creation only has reality in its contingent relation to the Creator.

Following on from Barth, we can regard the phrase as open to the interpretation that it is the symbolic language for the absolute negation, that which is so negative that it is beyond any concept of 'nothingness'; that which cannot be expressed (because all words have a relative content) in any suitable term. The outcome which it seeks to express is that there is only God and there is only what God wills.

The other part of the dilemma is that if we accept that God is a God of order, rationality and uncreated Light, a God who exists as divine order in the divine rationality of his triune existence in light unapproachable, how can this God produce that which is formless, chaotic and characterized by this particular darkness, if the *tohu-wabohu* is his first creative act? It is that which is contrary to his nature; it bears no correspondence to his uncreated existence and being in its created state. Indeed, how can formlessness have any existence at all? Perhaps we may extend a few thoughts suggested by Barth in this same passage of his *Church Dogmatics*, though not necessarily following his interpretation. We take our cue from his words[4]:

> ... we can turn again with fuller understanding to the dilemma whether the subject of v.2 – the primal and rudimentary state of the world – is self-originating or willed and posited by God. Our answer is that it is neither one nor the other. For the question of a primal and rudimentary state does not arise at all.

Tohu-wabohu and the *darkness* specifically mentioned here in these verses of Genesis, whatever the narrator had in mind, may be regarded from the vantage of the development of theological thought as a caricature, an attempt to draw verbally, that which God rejects – this nothingness which is qualitatively different from any nothingness we can even begin to imagine. It is this rejection over which the Spirit hovers – not the Creator Word – thus revealing it in its utter antithesis to God and the creative act and accomplishment of God. Certainly it can be an ever present threat to creation, but only as a threat to creation which rejects the Word as the author, sustainer and fulfiller of its existence. It is a description of that possible impossibility to which creation, with mankind at its heart, can turn, a Wordless existence. This utter nothingness which cannot be expressed is the alternative to the Word of God by whom all things are made, in whom they consist and for whom they were made. The myth of Genesis, therefore, is indeed a caricature of a world without the Word. God had not yet spoken and uttered his *fiat*, his *let there be.*

Second, with regard to all the interpretations noted by Augustine, what is meant by *heaven?* He engages in a survey of interpretations, which are acceptable to him as long as they do not compromise the utter primacy of God on whom all things other than Himself depend[5]. Out of this diversity of acceptable perspectives marshalled by Augustine, some later writers were to seize upon the idea that God creates, 'before' anything else, that heaven of heavens, that dimension where, as Augustine points out in his usage of the phrase coupled with *the intelligible heaven*[6]

> to understand is to know totally at once – not in part, nor darkly, not through a glass – but as an instantaneous totality in full perception, face to face.

That which immediately 'surrounds' God is created first, according to the mediaeval tradition. It is the heaven of light, approximating more closely than any other created entity to the uncreated Light which God is. It is that which is not as the sensible, corporeal creation, but consists of the light of pure intelligences, created as the first reflections of the uncreated Light.

It is not my purpose here to expound the text of Genesis. It is, rather, to suggest that the various commentators who have wrestled with it all have at least an implicit notion that light, whether it be in terms of an intelligible heaven the creation of which, as the first thing brought into being and not of itself liable to be described in temporal terms, is deduced in various ways from the text.

Their dilemma, from whatever angle they approach it, or textual construction they put upon it, centres round the diffi-

culty of even beginning the attempt to describe 'formlessness', and avoid the notion that God creates out of a pre-
existent substance which is co-eternal to himself because its
beginning cannot be explained. There seems to be an instinctive groping after the idea that nothing can exist unless light
be its determinative. 'Formlessness', I would suggest, is that
which the various commentators through the history of
Christian thought, in all that they say out of their various
and varied approaches, is a comment on the absence of light
and therefore of a state of affairs which is the negation of
creation. The words cluster around – *invisible, darkness, unwrought, unformed, chaos, void, gulf.* Whatever the original
narrator of Genesis had in mind, and whatever contemporary creation myths he drew on, with or without distinction,
his, and the whole subsequent exercise, is an attempt to
speak to a *creatio ex nihilo*, if not consciously as far as the
narrator's understanding is concerned, by speaking of the act
of creation as not compromising God who alone is Self-sufficient and by not according to creation, in its inception, that
which is contrary to its temporal/spatial nature, character
and identity.

We look now at the way in which some of these later
commentators, and particularly Basil, examine the Genesis
narrative in terms of light. Broadly speaking, interpreters of
Genesis would appear, by their varying emphases, to fall into
two categories: those who see formless matter as having first
place, and those who construe the text to indicate that light
holds that position. But there seems to be something of an
ambiguity amongst their writings and observations on the
place of light.

For example, the seventeenth century writer, John Swan,
can call light *God's eldest daughter*, yet deems that *In the
beginning God created the heavens and the earth* to mean[7]

> as if it should be said, These very heavens and this very earth,
> which now we see in being, were not always but began. Then
> afterwards ... speaking first how all was a disordered and
> deformed Chaos, the earth and the heavens not distinguished,
> but lying as it were in a confused heap all together. And this is
> manifest. For on the second day, when the heavens were
> made, it seemeth that there matter was from among that

masse or unfashioned lump which was said to be void and without form, and not able to be kept together, had not the Spirit of God cherished it, (for the spirit of God moving on the face of the waters, did as it were fit upon it and nourish it, as a fowl doth her egges, with heat and life) yea their matter, I say, was from among the waters, which by the power of Gods word were extended and stretched like a canopie round about the earth, as we now see them. In which regard S. Austines words are also pertinent ...

Swan is appealing to St Augustine: *Confessions, XII:21ff, XII:1ff*. Augustine had already stated in XII:8, that God created formless matter, and out of that brought form:

But this earth itself which you had made, was matter without form; it was invisible and without form, and darkness was over the abyss. From this formlessness which is almost nothing, you then made all things which make up the changeable world ...

St Basil, too, in his *Hexaemeron*[8], appears at first glance to take the same interpretation. It has to be noted that he is commenting on the Septuagint text of *Genesis 1:2*, where *without form and void* is translated from the Greek *invisible and unfinished*.

'The earth', says Holy Scripture, 'was invisible and unfinished'. The heavens and the earth were created without distinction ... What was the unfinished condition of the earth? And for what reason was it invisible? The fertility of the earth is its perfect finishing ... all of which, a little later, at the voice of God came forth from the earth to beautify her ... As nothing of all this yet existed, Scripture is right in calling the earth 'without form' ... The earth was invisible for two reasons. It may be that man, the spectator, did not yet exist, or because being submerged under the waters which overflowed the surface, it could not be seen ... What is invisible? First of all, that which our fleshly eye cannot perceive; our mind, for example; then that which, visible in its nature, is hidden by some body which conceals it, like iron in the depths of the earth. It is in this sense, because it was hidden under the waters, that the earth was still invisible. However, as light did not yet exist, and as the earth lay in darkness, because of the obscurity of the air above it, it should not astonish us that for this reason Scripture calls it 'invisible'.

It would seem that Basil does not regard light as the first act of creation; matter, invisible and unfinished, is.

However, in *Hexaemeron II:4,5*, he begins an examination of the statement *Darkness was upon the face of the deep*. In *Hexaermeron II:4*, he disposes of the idea that darkness refers to an evil power or the personification of evil in constant struggle with the God of light. In so doing, he removes the ground of the dualism at the heart of the Marcionite, Valentinian and Manichaean heresies. A definition of darkness is set out:

> air not illumined, the shadow produced by the intervention of a body, and lastly a place, for some reason, deprived of light.

No part of the earth was visible, not only because of the water covering it, but because the air around was deprived of light, and therefore not even a refracted glimpse of the earth through the water could be provided. Reasonable questions may be asked, notes Basil:

> Was darkness created with the world? Is it older than light? why, in spite of its inferiority, has it preceded it?

The answer to such is that darkness

> does not exist in essence; it is a condition produced in the air by the withdrawal of light.

Here an implicit note sounds out in Basil's commentary concerning the priority of light. The term *withdrawal* which he uses suggests that he is pointing to a prior light which is removed or removes. There then follows a passage, intriguing because it is ambiguous in the context of his earlier assertions.

> What then is the light which disappeared suddenly from the world, so that darkness should cover the face of the deep? If anything had existed before the formation of this sensible and perishable world, no doubt we conclude it would have been in light. The orders of the angels, the heavenly hosts, all intellectual natures named or unnamed, all the ministering spirits, did not live in darkness, but enjoyed a condition fitted for them in light and spiritual joy.

It would seem, on balance, that Basil is advocating the primacy of light in the supposed sequence of creation, not as an entity in itself but as the necessary nature of the heaven of God. This heaven is distinguished from the now visible heavens of *in the beginning God created the heavens and the earth*. In *Hexaemeron I:5*, he had already noted that

> it appears, indeed, that even before this world an order of things existed of which our mind can form an idea, but of which we can say nothing ... The birth of the world was preceded by a condition of things suitable for the exercise of supernatural powers, outstripping the limits of time, eternal and infinite. The Creator and Demiurge of the universe perfected His works in it, spiritual light for the happiness of all who love the Lord, intellectual and invisible natures, all the orderly arrangements of pure intelligences who are beyond the reach of our mind and of whom we cannot even discover the names.

It is to be remembered that Origen (c.185-c.254), whose exegetical thought and allegorical method stands behind that of Basil to some extent (not that Basil was without his criticism of Origen, as is instanced in his remarks in *De Spiritu Sancto: 73*), had claimed already in his *Homily I on Genesis*, and in his *Homily 4 on Isaiah*, that the angels, and therefore their *sphere* had existed *before the aeons*. He does, however, qualify this in *De Principiis, preface:10*, where in speaking of angels, he remarks

> When these, however, were created, or of what nature they are, or how they exist, is not clearly stated.

That there was a sphere other than that of this earth and its heavens and 'prior' in some sense to them, lies in conscious Christian tradition of the first centuries. Amongst Basil's contemporaries, Gregory of Nazianzen was more precise on the matter. In *Oration XXXVIII: 8,9*, he states that God first conceived the heavenly and angelic powers, a work fulfilled by his Word and perfected by his Spirit. These powers are

> secondary Splendours ... Ministers of the Primary Splendour [God himself as Father, Son and Spirit] ... illumined with the first rays from God – for earthly beings have but the second illumination.

The question of light and the orders of creation is here seen as a matter of qualitative difference in which, again, 'priority' is deemed to be the quality of degree of correspondence to, and participation in, that uncreated Light which God is. The 'world' of pure intelligences of light enjoys the quality of more intense communion with God as Light.

To this world, Basil claims it was necessary to add another world as a school for humanity. This is the visible, sensible universe in which we live and move and have our being. Basil is not advocating a heaven which is co-equal to God, and exists as he exists. All things other than God had a beginning, just as the earth and the heavens of the universe have a beginning. On that he is adamant. But this sphere of pure intelligences, while still created, is qualitatively different from the physical world with its heaven, which particular creation is characterized by its temporal/spatial nature, subject to change.

It must be emphasised that nowhere does Basil suggest that this 'sphere' of pure intelligences is beyond the universe in a spatial sense. Rather he emphasizes the qualitative difference, and that quality is beyond the mind with its measuring ability to grasp. Thus, when he uses the phrase *heaven of heavens* from *Psalm CXLVII:4*, appeals to that third heaven reported by St Paul in *II Corinthians XII:2*, and employs the statement with which he agrees that there is a *plurality of heavens*[9], he is not advocating a series of heavens either temporally or spatially superior, but adhering to that qualitative difference.

The point of this heaven 'preceding' is not a temporal statement. Basil makes much of the 'instantaneity' of the creative act of God – otherwise a temporal sequence is projected into the act, and therefore the being, of God:

> Thus then, if it is said 'In the beginning God created', it is to teach us that at the will of God the world arose in less than an instant, and it is to convey this meaning more clearly that other interpreters have said: 'God made summarily' that is to say, all at once and in a moment[10].

'Precedence' therefore takes on a meaning of 'qualitative comparison', rather than 'temporal priority'. Basil goes on to describe the heavens above the earth as that which in fact keeps out light from the earth.

When then, according to the order of God, enveloping all that
its circumference included, a vast and unbroken body separating outer things from those which it enclosed, it necessarily
kept the space inside in darkness for want of communication
with the outer light. Three things are, indeed, needed to form
a shadow, light, a body, a dark place. The shadow of heaven
forms the darkness of the world.

What is of note here is that the presence of light, albeit not
penetrating into the heaven above the earth and the earth
itself, is taken for granted. On the instantaneous action of
light, more will be said below. Here it suffices to note that
Basil accepts this peculiar motion of light in *Hexaemeron*
II:7 in commenting on God's creative command and act *let
there be light*.

In this section he proposes that light requires what he calls
the *aether* for its propagation, a premise that the later
Grosseteste, though familiar with Basil's *Hexaemeron*,
rejected, seeing light as self-sufficient. This too will be considered in a discussion of Grosseteste's significant thought
below, but Basil's point, for our purposes here, is that the
aether is so subtle that it allows the instantaneous diffusion
of light through the earth and the heavens above the earth.
This universal dispersal of light is accomplished because of
the sympathetic medium of the *aether*, which is so subtle and
transparent that it

needs not the space of a moment for light to pass through it.
Just as it carries our sight instantaneously to the object of
vision, so without the least interval, with a rapidity that
thought cannot conceive, it receives these rays of light in its
uttermost limits ... So, with a single word and in one instant,
the Creator of all things gave the boon of light to the world.

It may also be noted here that Grosseteste rejected the implicit idea that light moves from the eye to the object under
scrutiny, as Basil suggests here, and reversed the theory.

What Basil does in this section is to concentrate on the
aesthetics and effects of light, rather than on light itself. It
gives the world radiance, beauty and splendour. However,
the word he employs for 'beauty' – καλου – refers to the outward appearance of the inward condition which is construed
in terms of 'good' and 'integrity'. In other words, he is link-

ing the action of light to that of 'order'. The bestowal of beauty in this sense, harmony and order, is the nature of light. It is significant that Basil, in commenting on *Let there be light*, writes as his next words:

The first word of God created the nature of light.

I am tempted to conjecture that Basil interprets the first creative utterance of God as the illumination of the sensible world by that which is 'already' present in God's creative act in the realm of pure intelligences. This is not to postulate a distinction in Basil's thought between the world of things and the world of ideas, between the κοσμος νοητος and the κοσμος αισθητος, and that this disjunction indicates a dualistic interpretation. Though he sets out the sequence of creation in temporal form, and as in *Hexaemeron I:5*, it seems that he is advocating a temporal sequence wherein the world of pure intelligences is created first, nevertheless his insistence on the instant simultaneity of creation, and the nature of light in its role, hold both worlds together.

Light, for Basil, I would suggest, holds prior position in creation because of its quality which he tends to express in terms of its role. It is seated, as it were, in that 'realm' of pure intelligences, the heaven of God, created 'before' the heavens and the earth; that is, its source is that purity of rationality corresponding in its created quality more than anything else does or can, to the uncreated Rationality and Light which God is.

That (possibly 6th century) anonymous author, for long thought to be, and accepted as, the Dionysius the Areopagite mentioned in *The Acts of the Apostles*, but, after the dismissal of this theory, known as Pseudo-Dionysius, takes much the same theme to undergird his works. Undoubtedly familiar with the angelology of Gregory of Nazianzen, this writer's speculations on the 'realm' of pure intelligences of light 'above' this world of temporal/spatial dimension, had much influence, curiously more in the west than in his own eastern part of the church, in the matter of conjecture about this realm of light and on the hierarchical nature of its angelic existences of light. In western mediaeval thought, the post-Dionysian emphasis moved away from the nature of created light, either angelic or physical, to a gradation of degree of status as to the bearers of that light. As a result, the whole matter of light itself, its nature and quality, was displaced by secondary considerations born of speculation on quantitative prestige and dignity of rank within created orders.

However, the positive content of Pseudo-Dionysius's work must not be overlooked. Essentially, he is in his angelic speculation pointing to the outpouring of primal light in its relation to God as uncreated Light. His *hierarchies of angels* depend for their existence and offices on the divine *Hierarch*, God himself. The important factor in his thought must not be lost in shrinking away from his more obscure speculations, and that factor is that we have to do here with revelation – the way of mental illumination and information in order to know God in his Word as the Light which gives reason and purpose to all things and in whom, and for whom, and by whom, all things are. His observations on the *hierarchies* are dynamic interpretations of the function of light – even if some of his later commentators, and those who took the colour of their speculative theology from his work, introduced a more static interpretation.

Pseudo-Dionysius took the angelology of the first four centuries in Christian writing, particularly that of Gregory of Nazianzen, and used what was presumably his training in, and his undoubted adherence to, Neo-Platonic insights, as the handmaid both of scriptural texts and Patristic expositions of the subject of light and angels and revelation.

For Pseudo-Dionysius, the world of the light of angelic hierarchies has the priority over this world of spatial/temporal realities – but is not divorced from it. Its priority consists in its 'proximity' to God, in terms not of measurement but of *more generous communion* with him, its graded likeness to him, and its service to this creation[11].

> A hierarchy ... constantly looks directly at the ordered beauty of God. A hierarchy carries in itself the stamp of God. Hierarchy effectuates its members to be in every way images of God, to be clear and immaculate mirrors reflecting the radiance of primordial light, and, more, of God himself. It makes certain that when its members have been granted this

full and deiform splendour, that they then pass on this light unsparingly to beings lesser in rank in accordance to God's will.

This pouring out of light in its relation to God as Light is regarded by Pseudo-Dionysius as *providence*[12]. Moreover, all created things, even those with no life participate in it for their very existence. Those created with life, are the recipients of revelation because of this service of the angelic existences, and are thus 'lifted up', in the sense of 'illuminated', to God. It must be noted that for Pseudo-Dionysius, this is not some sort of alternative to the revelation of the Word made flesh. Indeed, the angelic existences depend for their existence on him, are the servants and announcers of him, and minister to the whole dispensation of that revelation[13]. The whole concept of 'hierarchy' and light is Christocentric. The fact that this is not stated at the beginning of Pseudo-Dionysius's work, and appears as only one section in the midst of much speculation, does not warrant a dismissal of its controlling importance. Christ is the Light of Light, and all other existences of light revolve round him. This Christocentricity is set out explicitly in terms of their communion with Christ and their primary participation in the knowledge of the *divine lights working out from him*[14].

The priority of the highest rank of the hierarchy of angelic intelligences is that they stand in the *anteroom of deity* – a Neo-Platonic term. This certainly indicates their creation 'prior' to this world and heaven of time and things, not in any temporal sense, but in degree of participation in and communion with God.

Light itself is given this prime position in *The Divine Names*[15] by Pseudo-Dionysius. His argument runs that, as the sun gives light to all things by virtue of its very existence and in its own way, so the goodness of God, the Archetype far beyond in excellence the light of the sun, sends out its rays to all things which thereby owe their existence to him. These are 'graded' according to their 'proximity' to, or, rather, their degree of participation in, this divine goodness, of which light is the visible image. The higher ranks lift up the lower in their distribution of this light. This light is distributed from God, the Cause of all who is beyond all in his transcendence. This process of distribution is completed when that Good, imaged by light, draws all things back to itself, gathering them together to itself, the Source and unifier of the totality of all creation. In it, they find their order and in its transcendence their fulfilment. This light is the measurer and counter of the hours and of all time. The implication is that all time, as the product of light, is gathered together in its relation to God as Light and Goodness.

We may well, through this, come to an idea of the recapitulation of all things and all time by virtue of the action of light as the image of God's goodness. The emphasis is not on temporal position of first, second, third, and so on in the creative sequence, but on gradation of quality through the action of light admitting to participation in, and communion with, God as Light and Good. Hence, time is not the measure of priority, but the bestowed quality of light in the things of time is. Priority in creation is found in the cyclical action of light, going from God through the levels of existences in differentiated quality of communion with him, gathering all, and returning. It is indeed an emphasis on dynamic quality rather than on temporal measurement. That light should be 'first' in the creative sequence is not the way that Pseudo-Dionysius approaches its significance. It is first because of its role and its relation to God and all other existences which he brings into being through that light. In a sense, light could not be construed as 'first' in any temporal construction of the word; it is 'precedent' in that it is with God, and, indeed, in his Word, is God, comes from God, and gathers up all things in itself.

The fact and the extent of the influence of Pseudo-Dionysius's work on the minds of the Middle Ages are not so clear cut and universal as, until quite recently had been thought. It has been all too often assumed that because the works were accepted as genuinely apostolic, the author's pseudonym generally being regarded as authentic, uncritical deference was accorded to them. Certainly, the number of translations, better translations, commentaries and treatises produced from the introduction of Pseudo-Dionysius's corpus of works in the west, until the 16th century show this. Some of the outstanding names producing these were

Hilduin, John Scottus Erigena, Sarrazin, Hugh of St Victor, Robert Grosseteste, Albert the Great, Thomas Aquinas and Bonaventure. The schools gave him place, and the practicalities of his influence may be instanced by the use of some of his ideas by Abbot Suger in the building of the basilica of Saint-Denis, Paris, in the first half of the 12th century. But there are surprizing instances of neglect. The monastic order, Benedictine, Cistercian and Carthusian, despite the facts that the works of Pseudo-Dionysius were represented well in its libraries, and various of its members, some illustrious, were commentators of his works, remained collectively and institutionally aloof from any fundamental and determinative influence of what is called his 'spirituality'. Only the Canons Regular in the 12th century were advocates of that, and the medium of the beginnings of his influence in later scholasticism from the 13th century.

The ambivalence within the mediaeval attitude towards Pseudo-Dionysius, either support for him or neglect of him without overt criticism, is perhaps best epitomized in Grosseteste's treatment of him particularly in the commentary on *The Celestial Hierarchy*. This approach we will be examining later in the consideration of Grosseteste's theology of light.

Suffice it to say in summing up Psuedo-Dionysius's legacy of thought, that his undoubted granting of cardinal position to the concept of light and to the pure intelligences, the beings of light, indicates that for him, light holds prime place in the understanding of the divine ordering of all things. The first section – 120A-121C – of *The Celestial Hierarchy* would, of itself, make this abundantly clear. Moreover, it is Christocentric in presentation.

By the fathers and authors cited above, I would suggest that even if the temporal sequence in which some of their commentaries are couched would seem to indicate that light for them was not regarded as the first creation of God, nevertheless, in the unfolding of theological thought, light occupies the prime place in creation, and is regarded in that sense as 'first'. The clear suggestion in so many writers is that time begins with the creation of light. But time and space are inseparably bound, and to create something – and therefore space, in that that something is given place – would seem logically to lead to the conclusion that there can be no existence, however 'formless' and inanimate, without light.

What then is the nature of this created light? Here I wish to turn to the work of Robert Grosseteste (c.1170-1253) entitled *De Luce: seu de Inchoatione Formarum – On Light: or on the Beginning of Forms*. Grosseteste was the first Chancellor of Oxford University and subsequently Bishop of Lincoln. His theological and scientific significance, standing out as it does in the whole sweep of mediaeval thought generally characterized by what is called 'scholasticism', has not been appreciated enough, despite the notable work done on him by Reidl, Crombie, McEvoy and Southern in their respective assessments. I believe that Grosseteste's contribution jumped over, as it were, his own time and, indeed, several subsequent generations. 'Before his time' is a commonplace with which he probably should not be labelled. The mind, in Grosseteste, is still mediaeval, But, like Duns Scotus and William of Occam, he perceived, by the very method he adopted in tackling his subjects, that what required reforming was the whole framework of mediaeval preconceptions of thought, if theological and scientific advance were to be made. Indeed, he was not above open criticism of prevailing trends: thus in his *De Cessatione Legalium III;2;1*, he argues against all philosophers influenced by Aristotle, who would claim that the world had no beginning. These

> Moses strikes and dashes to pieces with the blow of these words: In the Beginning.

His *modus operandi* in both theology and science (and the two were never in his mind separable) was to adopt a κατα φυσιν approach – that is to say, to let the object of his study reveal itself on its own terms and to discipline his mind to the nature of the object so revealing itself. This mode of thinking is removed from the philosophical subjectivism, born of one emphasis or another, which then prevailed. That that prevalence should prove, as it did largely, to stifle the possibility of a lasting influence of his works in their thought-reforming characteristics, in the generations immediately following

him, can only be regarded as an unfortunate lapse in granting place to a genuine wrestling with the nature of objective
truth, and as a set-back for such progress.

It is to his observations on, and the mode by which he
approaches, the subject of light in his treatise *De Luce* that
we now turn.

2
Translation of Grosseteste's *De Luce*

'The first bodily form, which some call corporeity, I deem to be light. For light, by itself, spreads itself in every direction, so that a sphere of light, however great you will, is generated instantly from a point of light, unless a barrier obstructs [its progress]. Certainly corporeity is that which the extension of matter into three dimensions necessarily accompanies, notwithstanding the fact that corporeity and matter must each in itself be a simple substance devoid of all dimension. But it would be impossible for a form which is in itself simple and devoid of dimension to bring dimension in every direction into matter similarly simple and devoid of dimension, unless it could multiply itself and spread itself instantly in every direction and in its own diffusion could extend matter, since form itself is not able to abandon matter, because it is not separable [from it], nor can matter itself be detached from form.

However, I have proposed light to be that whose own effect is this – namely to multiply its very self and extend instantly in every direction. Whatsoever, therefore, performs this work is either light itself or some working power participating to that degree in the light, which itself achieves this. Corporeity, therefore, is either light itself, or is that aforementioned power introducing dimensions into matter to the degree it participates in that same light and works through the property of the light. But, indeed, it is impossible that primary form itself should introduce dimensions into matter through the power of a subsequent form. Therefore light is not a form following from corporcity itself, but is itself corporeity.

Furthermore: the wise deem the first bodily form to be worthier than all subsequent forms and of more excellent and of more noble essence, and rather comparable to forms that exist separately. Indeed, light is of a more dignified, noble and excellent essence than all corporeal things, and rather to be compared to forms which are intelligences, standing separate from all bodies. Light, therefore, is the first corporeal form.

Thus light, which is the first form in first created matter, extended itself at the beginning of time, multiplying itself an infinity of times through itself on every side and stretching out equally in every direction, dispersing with itself matter, which it was not able to desert, to such a great mass as the fabric of the cosmos. An extension of matter could not be achieved by a finite multiplication of light because a simple thing does not beget finitely as great a replica of itself, as Aristotle demonstrated in *De Caelo et Mundo*. Indeed it is necessary to beget a certain finite thing by multiplying an infinity of times because the production of any thing by infinite multiplication exceeds the thing infinitely, out of whose multiplication it is produced. Indeed, a simple thing is not exceeded by a simple thing infinitely, but a certain finite thing alone exceeds a simple thing infinitely. For something infinite exceeds a simple thing an infinity of times infinitely. Therefore, light – which is itself a simple thing – multiplied an infinity of times is necessary to extend matters (likewise simple) in dimensions of finite bulk.

On the other hand, it is possible that an infinite numerical sum itself is constituted as the infinite summing up in every numerical proportion and even every non-numerical [proportion]. And some infinities are larger than others, and others are smaller. The sum of all numbers, whether even or odd, is infinite, and so it is greater than the sum of all even numbers, although this, nonetheless, is infinite – for it exceeds it by the sum of all uneven numbers. Furthermore, the sum of numbers doubled from one onwards is infinite, and likewise the sum of all numbers halved corresponding to these doubles is infinite. The sum of these halves must of necessity be half the sum of their doubles. In the same way, the sum of all numbers from one, tripled, is three times the sum of all the thirds answering to these triples. And this is likewise evident concerning all sorts of proportioned numbers, since – in accordance with whatever of them you will – there can be a proportion from infinite[1] to infinite.

But if there is considered [both] the infinite sum of all doubles from one onwards and the infinite sum of all halves corresponding to these doubles, and if one, or any other finite number, is taken away from the sum of the halves, then after the process of subtraction there will no longer be a two to one proportion between the first sum and the remainder of the second sum – nor yet any other numerical proportion at all, since if from a numerical proportion there is to be left by subtraction from the lesser end[2] another numerical proportion, it is necessary that the subtraction should be an aliquot part or several aliquot parts [of the sum] from which it is subtracted. And a finite number cannot be an aliquot or aliquots of an infinite number. Therefore, when a number has been subtracted from the infinite sum of halves, no numerical proportion may be left between the infinite sum of doubles and the remainder of the infinite sum of halves.

Therefore these things being so, it is plain that light by its infinite multiplication extends matter into smaller finite dimensions and into larger finite dimensions according to whatever proportion they have with each other, that is, numerical and non-numerical. For if light by its infinite multiplication extends matter into a double dimension, by the same infinite multiplication doubled it extends it into a quadruple dimension, and, by the same halved, it extends it into a single dimension, and so according to other proportions, numerical and non-numerical.

This, as I think, was understood of those philosophers maintaining everything to be composed from atoms, and saying bodies were composed from surfaces and surfaces from lines and lines from points. Nor does this conclusion contradict it, which maintains magnitude to be composed only from magnitudes, because the whole is described by as many ways as is the part. For in different ways the half is called part of the whole, which, doubled, produces the whole, and the side is part of a diameter which does not produce the [whole] diameter [even if it be] multiplied any number of times, but [being so] multiplied any number of

1. As in MSS R,D,P,V: MSS M,a, and Baur have 'finitum'
2. That is, from the end of the lesser infinite number, the infinite sum of the halves.

times is [always] exceeded by the diameter. And in different ways, an angle of a contingency[1] is called part of a right angle in which it is an infinite number of times, and yet finitely subtracted from [the angle, it] diminishes it, and a point is called part of a line in which [it] is an infinite number of times, and a finite subtraction from [the line] does not diminish it.

Returning then to my argument, I say that light, by making its own infinite multiplication equally in every direction, extends matter everywhere equally into a spherical form, and there necessarily follows from this extension that the further parts of matter are more stretched out and more rarefied than those parts within, next to the centre. And if the extremities were rarefied as much as possible, still the interior parts would be susceptible to greater rarefication.

Light, therefore, by extending primary matter in this way into a spherical form and rarefying the extremities as much as possible, completed the potentiality of matter in the outward sphere, nor did it leave it susceptible to further impression. And thus the primary body is perfected in the extremity of that sphere which is called the firmament, having nothing in its composition except primary matter and primary form. And therefore it is a most simple body, as far as the parts constituting its essence and the greatest quantity, not differing from the generic body except insomuch only as in it matter is completed by primary form. Indeed, the generic body which is in this and in other bodies, containing in its essence primary matter and primary form, detracts from the fulfilment of matter by primary form and from the diminution of matter by primary form.

Therefore, when that primary body which is the firmament has been completed in this way, it spreads light from every part of itself into the centre of everything. For, since light is the perfection of the primary body, which naturally multiplies itself from the primary body, light necessarily spreads itself into the centre of everything – which, since the whole form is not separable from matter in its diffusion from the primary body, extends with itself the spiritual quality of

---

1. The angle made by a tangent with the circumference of a circle.

the matter of the primary body. And so there proceeds from the primary body light, which is a spiritual body, or rather a corporal spirit. This light in its passage does not divide the body through which it passes, and it penetrates instantly from the primary body of heaven as far as the centre. Nor is its passage such as if any one thing were to be understood by measure passing instantly from heaven into the centre – for this perhaps is impossible – but its passage is through its multiplication and infinite generation of light. Therefore this light, spread from the primary body into the centre, also gathered a compressed mass existing within the primary body; and since the primary body could not now be reduced – that being complete and invariable – nor could the place become void – it was necessary that the outward parts of the mass in that convergence should be extended and separated. And thus greater density originated in the interior parts of this mass, and in the exterior parts sparseness was increased; and the power of the light converging and that [of the light] separating in that convergence was such that [these powers] made those exterior parts of the mass contained within the primary body to the greatest extent more subtle and more rarefied. And thus a secondary sphere was formed capable of receiving no further impression in those exterior parts of this mass. And such is the fulfilment and perfection of the secondary sphere; the light indeed is produced from the primary sphere, and the light, simple in the primary sphere, is duplicated in the secondary sphere.

As, however, the light born from the primary sphere formed the secondary sphere and left a more dense mass within the secondary sphere, so the light born from the secondary sphere completed a tertiary sphere, and within that tertiary sphere left, by [its] convergence, a still more dense mass. And in this order this convergence proceeded to disperse, until the nine celestial spheres were formed, and there had gathered below[1] the ninth interior sphere a thickened mass which was the matter of the four elements. But this interior sphere – which is the sphere of the moon – even

---

1. Reading 'infra' instead of Baur's 'intra'

begetting light from itself, concentrated by its light the mass contained within itself, and with this concentration it thinned and dispersed its exterior parts. However, the power of this light was not such that with the concentration it dispersed its exterior parts totally. Therefore imperfection remained in every part of this mass and the possibility of reception of convergence and dispersal. And the last part of this mass, not having been dispersed to the utmost, however, by its dispersal [when] accomplished, fire, the matter of the elements still remained. And this element, begetting light from itself and concentrating a mass contained within itself, dispersed its exterior parts, with, however, less dispersal of the fire itself; and thus it produced fire. Indeed, fire begetting light from itself and concentrating a mass contained within, dispersed its exterior parts, with however less dispersal of itself; and thus it produced air. Air also, generating from itself a spiritual body or a corporal spirit, and concentrating [it] contained within itself and by this concentration dispersing its externals, produced water and earth. But because in water more remained of the concentrating virtue than the dispersing, likewise water itself, with earth, remained heavy.

In this way, therefore, the thirteen spheres of this sensible world were brought into being – namely nine celestial, immutable, not susceptible to enlargement, reproduction and corruption, as being complete, and four existing in the opposite way, mutable and susceptible to enlargement, reproduction and corruption, as being incomplete. And it is clear how much any higher body, according to the light begotten from itself, is the specific form and perfection of the next body. And just as unity in potentiality is every subsequent number, so the primary body through the multiplication of its light is every subsequent body.

Earth, however, is all higher bodies, through the collection in itself of higher lights. Therefore it is itself what is, by the poets, called 'Pan', that is 'everything'; and the same 'Cybele', as it were a bed, is named from 'cubo', that is, 'solidity'[1], because she is of all bodies the most dense, that is

---

1. 'Cubo' is a peculiar word, related to the verb 'I lie down', 'I lay something down', 'I place', or to 'a cube'.

Cybele, mother of all the gods, because, while in her higher lights are collected, they however have not originated in her by their own operations, but it is possible that light can be derived from her in action and operation of whatever sphere you will, and thus from her, as if from some mother, any one at all of the gods will be begotten. However, their intermediate bodies are so disposed in two particulars. For indeed, truly, they are so disposed to the inferior ones as is the primary heaven to all those remaining [other than it] and to the superior ones, as earth to all the others. And thus in various ways in any one of them all the rest exist.

And the form and perfection of all bodies is light; but of the superior bodies rather spiritual and simple, of the inferior bodies, however, rather corporeal and multiplied[1]. Nor are all bodies of the same sort, though they may be produced by light simple or multiplied, just as numbers are not of the same sort, while, however, they may be derived from unity by greater or lesser multiplication.

And in this exposition is strongly apparent the meaning of those who say 'all things are one by the perfection of the one light', and the meaning of those who say 'things which are multifarious are multifarious by the diverse multiplication of the same light'.

When, however, inferior bodies share in the form of the superior bodies, the inferior body, by sharing of this same form with the superior body, is capable of motion by the same incorporeal motive virtue, by which motive virtue the superior body is moved. On account of this, the incorporeal virtue of intelligence or soul, which moves the primary and highest sphere by the day's motion, moves all inferior celestial spheres by the same day's motion. But by how much they are inferior so much more weakly do they receive this motion, because by however much it may be an inferior sphere, so much less pure and weaker is the primary corporeal light in it.

But though the elements may share in the form of the primary heaven, they are not, however, moved by the motive

---

1. In the sense of 'complex'.

force of the primary heaven by the day's motion. Although they share that primary light, they do not, however, conform to the primary motive virtue, since they possess that light impure, weak, extended from its purity in the primary body and since they possess moreover a density of matter which is the cause of resistance and non-conformity. But some think that the sphere of fire is moved around by the day's motion, and they advance as a sign of this the rotation of the comets, and say that even this motion is drawn so far as to the waters of the seas, so that from it proceeds the tidal change of the seas. Nevertheless all those philosophizing rightly say that the earth is immune from this motion.

In the same way, too, the spheres which are after the secondary sphere, which usually to the computation made above are named as eight, because they share in its form, all join in their motion which they have proper [to each] besides the day's motion.

But [as for] these same celestial spheres, because they are complete [and] not liable to thinning or thickening, the light in them does not draw the parts of matter *from* the centre to thin them, but *to* the centre to thicken [them]. And because of this, those celestial spheres are not liable to motion upward or downward, but only to a circular motion by their intelligent motive virtue, which in itself corporeally reflecting an angular distance, turns those spheres by corporeal rotation. But [as for] the elements because incomplete [and therefore??] liable to thinning or thickening, the light in them tends either from the centre to thin or to the centre to thicken. And because of that they are naturally mobile either upward or downward.

But in the first body, which is the simplest of bodies, one can find four [qualities], that is form, matter, ordering and what is ordered. Now form, being the most simple, obtains the place of unity. But matter, because of its twofold potential – that is, susceptibility to impressions and receptibility of them – and even because of its density, which fundamentally is [the nature] of this matter, which first and principally occurs through duality, is allotted deservedly a nature of duality. But composition contains a triple nature in itself, ordered in each [entity] for in it there is apparent matter made form, and form made material, and its own property of ordering[1], which is found as a third from both matter and form.

And what is ordered besides these three properties, is described under a quadruple number.

There is therefore in the primary body – in which, that is, all other bodies are present virtually – a quadruple quality, and therefore, fundamentally, the number of other bodies is not found [to be] beyond ten. For the unity of form and the duality of matter and the triple quality of order and the quadruple quality of what is ordered when they are added together, make ten[2]. This is why ten is the number of the bodies of the sphere of the world, for though the sphere of the elements may be divided into four, it is, however, one through sharing of corruptible worldly nature.

From these things it is plain that ten is the perfect number of universality, because it has within itself everything complete and perfect – in some respect like form and unity, and in some respect like matter and duality, and in some respect like order and a triple quality, and in some respect like what is ordered and a quadruple quality. Nor does it happen [that one needs] to add a fifth besides these four. Thus ten is everything complete and perfect.

From these things it is also manifest that only the five proportions found in these four numbers – one, two, three, four – are fitted for the ordering and establishing of concord in everything ordered. Therefore only these five harmonious proportions are present in musical modulations, melodies and rhythmic tempi.

[Thus] unfolds the tract On Light of the bishop of Lincoln.'

---

1. Assuming in this translation that in the Baur text 'in unoquoque compositio' agrees with 'ternarium', 'the triple nature'.
2. c.f. the 13th century heraldic device of ten roundels in a shield placed in lines of four, three, two, and one, graded downwards.

3

Light: the first of all forms; Comment on Grosseteste's *De Luce*

Date:

The composition of this short work may be dated between 1235 and 1241. The mature and deliberative nature of its contents suggests that it is one of Grosseteste's later rather than, as McEvoy advocates[1], earlier works. Southern stands by a later date on the grounds of the evolution in Grosseteste's thinking from the level of the understanding he had achieved compared with that in his *Hexaemeron. De Luce*, in Southern's view, even if it

> tails away into a rather chaotic and unintelligible sequel in its final paragraphs

yet is

> one of the most lucid and brilliantly conceived pieces of writing of Grosseteste's last years[2].

Southern would date the *Hexaemeron* at 1232-1233. He sees a development in Grosseteste's ideas about light from its

> more confused and incomplete

treatment in that work, via its *tentative form* in *De Operantionibus Soli*, to its full fruition in *De Luce*.[3]

McEvoy, on the other hand, argues that the more superficial treatment of light in the *Hexaemeron* and *De Operantionibus Soli* is not due to undeveloped thought, but that these works had different and more limited purposes and objectives. This I find surprising on the grounds of the importance accorded by Grosseteste to light in the whole act of creation and the necessary deduction from this that, had the *Hexaemeron* been the later work, his expounding of the creation of light would have been far less slight. Southern counters McEvoy's claim on the textual arguments of

Grosseteste's employment of previous written material, for example from his *Commentary on the Psalms*, in the *Hexaemeron*. If *De Luce* was earlier than the *Hexaemeron*, he already had a corpus of material on light from which he would undoubtedly have drawn for the composition of the *Hexaemeron*, either quoting from it or summarizing it. There is not one hint of this.

It may be taken that the observations of light presented in *De Luce* reflect, in the surer grasp and stronger understanding of the subject, Grosseteste's maturely considered conclusions.

The outlook of De Luce

Grosseteste states his findings definitively, and, while some Aristotelian terms are used, these are not the conveyors of Aristotelian substance of thought, but rather, they are bent out of their accustomed philosophical usage to serve what emerges as Grosseteste's originality of perception. The one reference to Aristotle's *De Caelo et Mundo* only heightens this, for the reference is used by Grosseteste merely as a stirrup to mount himself aloft on other themes, in this case his own understandings of relative infinities and their significance for light. Moreover, the divergence between his thought and that of Aristotelianism is seen in one of his fundamental theses here, namely that matter is not pure potency according to Grosseteste, but possesses innately a primordial, simple reality. Again, his statement in *De Luce*, that there is

> a first corporeal form

ushers in a decidedly non-Aristotelian tenet of a plurality of forms.

The general tenor of the method and presentation of this work is decidedly 'unscholastic' and free of any shackles of Aristotelian predispositions or strictures. For overall there is a method of thinking κατα φυσιν, that is to say, an objective way of thinking which does not approach the object of its study with preconceptions based on another authority other than that which is the object's own, or on the mind's supposed autonomy, but allows the object, from what it is in itself, to inform the mind and conform the mind's processes to its objective nature. This process of objective thinking evolves in Grosseteste's writings and is found in fully developed form in *De Luce*. It is an observational mode of thought, but not one of mere surface scrutiny concerned with external form alone. Rather, it grapples in obedient perception with the totality of the nature of the object, both what it substantially is in itself and what it is in relation to other realities. In this case, the object of study is light.

The precise presentation of his argument with all certainty and clarity displays a mind taking its own path with a confidence not in itself, primarily, but on the basis of what it has learned from faithfulness to the object itself. Such confidence is not apparent in the more tentative approach to the subject of light in both the other works where light figures largely – *De Operationibus Soli*, somewhat less hesitatingly than the *Hexaemeron*, but nevertheless still less definitively than *De Luce*.

De Luce seems to represent a final stage both in Grosseteste's way of thinking, the general method of approach to the object of his study which is more akin to our approach in natural science than that of his contemporaries, and in the particular progression of his exploration of light, its nature and properties, and its role in creation. We may add further to the question of the dating of this work that, on these grounds, Southern's view of this as a more mature and developed theological and scientific work is to be preferable to McEvoy's earlier dating.

The scope of De Luce

The first section of the treatise is bounded by the phrase at the beginning and repeated at the close:

> formam primam corporalem: the first corporeal form.

In this section, the nature and properties of light are set out succinctly. The instantaneous and omnidirectional diffusion of light is emphasized together with its role in this action with regard to matter to which it is bound as the first and most exalted corporeal form. Its excellence lies in the fact that it bears closer affinity to those pure forms, the intelligences – that is to say, the heavenly beings who, in the quality of their existence of created light apart from matter, are more correspondent to God than any other created actuality.

Light at creation is a simple substance lacking all dimension. So is matter. Although Grosseteste writes of light and matter as two entities, they are, in his view, inseparably conjoined: they cannot exist independently of each other. Hence, light is *the first bodily form*. Matter of and by itself, as a primordial point of creation, cannot effect anything. It is unproductive, impotent. Of and by itself it is of no moment for the evolution of creation. *Simple substance*, as applied to matter, is a term read back from the present state of matter as it has developed into its full, present existence and state, as a convenient theory to set out the nature of the first creative act of creation and the process involved thereafter.

Moreover, although he treats light and matter as theoretically separate, in that he mentions them apart, he is more concerned with the nature of things as they are in themselves, which, as he sees it, is the union of light and matter. It is this union of first form and first matter which is significant and on which the rest of his commentary rests. For he looks at light also as a *simple substance*, devoid of dimension but instantly dynamic, that which is the first form of matter and on which matter to be productive utterly depends.

This fits in with Grosseteste's general scheme of calculation concerning infinities set out in the second section of *De Luce*. Here, his mathematics concern those substances, light and matter, which in the beginning, or as the beginning, have no dimension. The mathematics of infinity on the one hand are the same as those which hold for *simplicity* on the other.

The mathematical term *simple*, employed by Grosseteste here, requires elucidation. By it, he means that that to which it is applied is *uncomplicated*: it is not anything other than what it is in itself. It indicates a fundamental essence of such nature and quality that it has no weight, dimension or attribute other than that of a point – that is, it designates *place but no measurement*.

Here the parallel to Grosseteste's mathematics of infinity is clear. Both *simple* and *infinite* are at the ends of the qualitative spectrum. They are not conclusive measurements as such, but terms employed at the boundaries of the mind's capacity and ability to point to the rationale of what lies between them, as it were.

The implicit mathematics concerning that which is *simple* is that a simple substance of no dimension plus another simple substance of no dimension will merely make one composite substance – in this case primal light or corporeity and primal matter – still simple and of no dimension. This is of significance, for it means that for Grosseteste the singularity at creation is light or corporeity and matter together, not separately.

The question does not arise here for Grosseteste as to whether light or matter was the product of the first divine act of creation. There is no question in this treatise of Grosseteste hazarding the view that unformed matter was created first, then light following as a later act of creation on the part of God. He emphasises in the clearest possible way that form cannot be divorced from matter, nor matter from form. We are left with Grosseteste's implied, but definite, conclusion that light and matter are instantaneously created. But light has the priority in so far as it is the potent and active form of matter. Indeed, it is the purest matter possible. There is no eulogizing, no cataloguing the aesthetics of light here as there is in the *Hexaemeron*. We are faced with a logical catalogue of unadorned statements – the unfolding of his understanding of natural facts.

His assertion that form or light and matter cannot exist without each other would seem to indicate that he assumes a simultaneous creation of form and matter in the one composite yet (though not contradictory in his mathematics) simple, primal point. In any case, as we will see, his view of an instantaneous creation is set out in his consideration of the nature of the six days of creation in the context of the light of angelic cognitions of the order of God's handiwork in his *Hexaemeron*. What is of immediate import here is that light and matter are viewed in their unity in such a way that in the remainder of *De Luce* he treats matter only in terms of light and light only in terms of the purest matter. We may also add here that matter without form would be non-existent. It is totally irrational to say that matter is 'formless'. It may not have a strictly geometrically recognizable form, but some sort of form, it must have. Grosseteste recognizes this in insisting on the indissoluble union between matter and form. But what sort of form can that which has place but no measurement, have?

Here we must turn to a consideration of what Grosseteste means by *form*. We have noted already his discarding of an Aristotelian usage of the term. And behind that jettisoning there lies a difference in concept.

Corporeity is the first form of creation. *Form* does not indicate 'shape' or 'surface contours' in the first instance. It betokens 'dynamic order' or 'ordered energy'. Corporeity, as the first form created, is itself the order and movement of all matter. It is more than 'potential', for it is realized potential in its nature and action, and only as this is it the 'shape' of things. Moreover, it is, by its nature and action, the disposer of all things in their relation one to another. Not only is it the dynamic order or ordered energy of each thing as it is in itself, but it is this too of the totality of creation and therefore the 'how' of the relation of each thing to all the others which compose creation. Form is concerned both *in se* and *ad extra*. That alone which has such a nature and an action is, in Grosseteste's analysis and conclusion, light. The universe is therefore a universe of light, and the existence of each entity composing it as a totality of entities, is characterized by light.

Only light, the first, the purest, swiftest corporeal form, and no subsequent (and therefore lower and less perfect) form, could accomplish such movement, dispersal, identity and order. For

> Light is of a more dignified, noble and excellent essence than all corporeal things, and rather to be compared to forms which are intelligences.

Created light corresponds more closely to the pure and spiritual intelligences which are totally apart from created matter in this dimension of creation. It is not an extension of uncreated Light (which can only be God himself, or a 'form' (in the Aristotelian sense) of it.

> *Quapropter Deus, qui lux est, ab ipsa luce cuius tanta est dignitas merito inchoavit sex dierum opera.*

> Wherefore, God who is light, by that self-same light which is assuredly the dignity of all things, laid the foundation of the six days' work.[4]

The context of this quotation from the *Hexaemeron* makes the distinction between the Light which God is and created light, abundantly clear. This latter light corresponds in its created nature and quality to that Light which calls it into existence, and in that correspondence and subsequent rational ordering of all things, echoing again in the created dimension that Rationality and Order which God is in his Triune Being, is the mutual harmony of all things with each other and all with God.

Light is the sublime conjunction between creation and Creator. In his treatment of light both in *De Luce* and in the *Hexaemeron* in which he eulogizes it, he underlines its unique place in the universe, and the nature of its properties he sees as a pointer to the truth of God. Its constant being, its self-integrity, its universal action, its unceasing function, its fundamental role by which all things are dependent upon it, its direct pathway as it moves rationally in straight lines with geometric precision – all these he sees as paradeigmatic qualities pointing beyond themselves to the nature of God who is Light himself.

With regard to the action of light, its inseparable relation to matter means that it bestows on matter dimension, direction, movement and order.

> Certainly corporeity is that which the extension of matter into three dimensions necessarily accompanies.

Only the action of light, which by nature instantly multiplies itself and diffuses itself in every direction, can be the agent and reality of such an extension. It draws matter with itself in its movement equally spread in every direction from that primordial point, determines the differing qualities of matter, disperses matter quantitatively, disposes matter according to the nature of these qualities, and orders all things, so brought into their identities, in their relation one with another, to the totality of them, and to itself.

This movement is from that primordial point of place but no dimension, which we may well call a 'singularity' in modern terms, out equally in every direction until it reaches that distance where it is so rarefied that movement ceases. This limit where cessation occurs forms a perfect sphere, and the circumference of this sphere is, in Grosseteste's view, the firmament. The universe is perceived by him to be spherical, and it is a sphere where light has dispersed matter and ordered it.

But what is the nature of this movement? Grosseteste tackles this question mathematically and the second section sets out these the mathematics of this action of light. This is a most significant development in thought, for there is implied clearly an advanced concept of relative infinities. It is true that such a concept can be found in, for example, Augustine of Hippo, and , indeed, before him in certain Greek mathematicians. But this concept is drawn out by Grosseteste in a way in which the mathematics are made to serve the dynamic reality of light, rather than, as was so often previously the case, the mathematics being the framework into which the realities were fitted and judged accordingly. The concept 'infinity' became a rigid mental instrument of judgment. With Grosseteste, the dynamic realities are never made subservient to conceptually static theories. His mathematics centre here round the 'actualization' of a simple being, that is, the 'extension' of that singularity which has existence but no dimension. The creation of all is a matter of the extension of that singularity, which is 'simple', into finite realities. That extension from simple to finite requires an infinite multiplication, for a finite thing exceeds a simple thing infinitely.

Grosseteste's particular employment of mathematical concepts in his writings, but especially in *De Luce*, in looking at the doctrine of creation and its attendant issues, is noteworthy. This is a consistent theme of his, for, as he remarks of God:

> *iste est mensurator primus et certissimus.*
> so He is the prime and most certain Mathematician.[5]

In the *Commentaries in VII Libros Physicorum Aristotelis*, the burden of his argument is that what is infinite to us is finite to God. This has fundamental implications for the

dynamic relation of creation to Creator, perceived by
Grosseteste and here expressed mathematically, as a contingent relation to and from God who is over and beyond all
measurement, but who

    omnia creavit in numero, pondere et mensura.
    created all things in number, weight and measure.[6]

But only God, who is alone Infinite, can initiate and accomplish this action of bringing finite things out of the simple by
what is, to us, infinite ways of working that out. The agent
he uses is light, so that his infinite multiplication of light –
remembering that infinities are relative to each other –
accomplishes the various and varied dimensions of matter
into identifiable bodies with their respective identities and
quantities and qualities.

The third section concerns this shape and quality of the
universe determined by the movement and diffusion of light,
infinitely multiplying itself equally in all directions from its
primordial and simple point, and extending matter with itself
in so doing. This, and Grosseteste's subsequent description of
the universe, prefigures, even in its mediaeval tone, what has
come to be known as the 'Big Bang' theory. Likewise, in the
matter of the respective density and rotation of the spheres
created in and by this action of light, there is an embryonic
suggestion of the principle of gravity. Again, the supposedly
modern ideas of levels of relative existences interpenetrating
one another, so that the lower field depends on the higher, is
foreshadowed:

> *Cum autem corpora inferiora participant formam superiorem*
> *corporum, corpus inferius participatione eiusdem formae cum*
> *superiore corpore est reciptivum motus ab eadem virtut*
> *emotiva incorporali, a qua virtute motiva movetur corpus*
> *superius.*
> When, however, inferior bodies share in the form of superior
> bodies, the inferior body by sharing of this same form with
> the superior body is capable of motion by the same incorpo-
> real motive virtue, by which motive virtue the superior body
> is moved.

The first observations of Grosseteste in the first section
concerning the mode of the ordering of the universe, are

repeated and elaborated. This ordering is determined by the character, quality and action of light. It is the property of light to expand instantaneously in every direction from a pin point *devoid of dimension* to a sphere, as he notes in the first section, the size of which sphere is determined by the potency of light, as light spreads omnidirectionally until it is so rarefied that It can move no further.

It is to be noted that there is no question in this treatise of Grosseteste hazarding the view that: Light does not require another agent to realize its potency or assist in its action. This self-sufficiency of light is one of the original tenets of Grosseteste. Here he parts company with Basil's way of setting out the bringing into being of aspects of creation as a temporal sequence following the development of the biblical narrative, by emphasizing the independent sufficiency of light. This presentation following the temporal sequence of the development of the creation narrative in Genesis, in Basil's faithfulness to the text on which he is commenting. As suggested above (chapter 1), this is perhaps to be interpreted in the context of his emphasis on priority of quality, rather than in terms of literal temporal precedence.

Here in *De Luce*, Grosseteste will have nothing to do with what even the faithfulness of Basil's commentary to the literal sequence of the Genesis text, suggests: namely that there is a temporal sequence of acts of creation in which light does not hold the prime position. Light has the priority; there is no previous heaven and earth predating it. In other words, the implication is clear that for Grosseteste, time begins with the creation of light – indeed that without light and its dynamic character there could not be time.

He does, however, follow Basil in respect of the instantaneous action of light and the extent of that action. The latter notes, in his comments on the divine command *Let there be light*, in his *Hexaemeron*[7]:

> The air was lighted up, or rather, made the light circulate mixed with its substance, and distributing its splendour rapidly in every direction, so dispersed itself to its extreme limits ... Up it sprang to the very aether and heaven. In one instant it lighted up the whole extent of the world ... For the

aether also is such a subtle substance and so transparent that it needs not a moment for light to pass through it. Just as it carries out sight instantaneously to the object of vision, so without the least interval, with a rapidity that thought cannot conceive, it received these rays of light in its uttermost limits.

The difference and the similarities between Basil and Grosseteste are obvious. The insistence on the instantaneity of light's action and effect is employed and developed by Grosseteste. Basil's claim that the air is the medium which light utilizes for its movement is over-ruled and rejected. Clearly, Grosseteste dismisses any such notion that light requires a medium other than its own potency for it to be operative.

It may also be remarked on again that Grosseteste in his writings dealing with the science of optics, also parts company from Basil in the matter of light coming from the object to instruct the eye, which is the opposite of Basil's understanding of light and sight proceeding from the eye to the object.

Light (*lux*) from its primordial point extends instantly in every direction, taking matter with it, to its extreme of rarefaction. This extreme, by the action of light so multiplying itself instantly in every direction, is a sphere which is the first and highest body. This sphere reflects light (*lumen*) inwards and, as it proceeds inwards in increasing density of matter, it creates the second sphere, inside which, by its like reflection from this sphere's bounds, it creates the third sphere, and so on until its extremity of density is reached.

The highest body, the firmament, is perfect, because in its rarefaction there is simplicity. The subsequent spheres are less and less so, and it is their graded density which gives them their characteristics and place in the whole cosmic spread caused by the action of light.

Whatever we may make of this scientifically, it does reach towards an objective attempt to analyse what constitutes the unity and diversity of creation and the relational entities within its total sphere, and to give a rational resolution of the significance of that unity and diversity from the highest, first and simplest body, the firmament

in quo scilicet virtualiter cetera corpora sunt
in which, that is, all other bodies are present virtually

to all the other bodies as they exist in the subsequent spheres, down to the sphere of earthly elements. All bodies are actualized and qualified as light is qualified in its procession of instant generation and multiplication of itself.

In the already quoted excerpt from the *Hexaemeron*[8]

Quapropter Deus, qui lux est, ab ipsa luce cuius tanta est dignitas merito inchoavit sex dierum opera:
Wherefore God, who is light, by the selfsame light which assuredly is the dignity of all things, laid the foundation of the six days' work.

– we have the view that light is created in correspondence to the uncreated Light which God is. In its rationality, which is its created correspondence to the uncreated rationality of God, it is the order of creation, the harmony of the universe, the beauty of nature, the perfection of art and the dignity of things seen and unseen. Thus in such aesthetic appreciation, spread throughout the writings of Grosseteste, light is eulogized. But in *De Luce* comes the mature and considered reason for this estate and dignity of light and its effects, and this last section of this work – the unity and unifying role of light, the composition, diversity, characteristics and qualities of created bodies, the potential of these entities in their relation one to another and one to all, and the questions of perfection and corruptibility – addresses this.

The fourth section undoubtedly appears awkward and difficult, but if it is placed in the context of all that Grosseteste says about light and the firmament, the first and highest body of all creation, to which all other bodies down to the elements are related in a harmonious relativity, and how he views the smallest entity as a dynamic identity related to that self-same light, then the logic in his thoughts here perhaps can be grasped. Light is the bond and characteristic of all creation. Multiplicity emerges from its simplicity, diversity from its unity. With this in view, while Grosseteste doubtlessly rounds off his thesis in the accepted contemporary manner of speculation on the perfect number, this is no mere stylistic finish demanded by custom. He has eschewed empty formality by bending it to serve all that he has written in the previous sections with regard to light as the ground of perfection and the foundation of the stability of existence in diversity, as it really is in itself in the creative purpose of God.

4

The Constancy of Created Light and the Nature of God

GROSSETESTE'S perception of the relation between light and matter is a remarkable foreshadowing of how that relation is presently and scientifically understood. In his insistence on the inextricable union of light and matter, that light is that dynamic which fulfils the potentiality of matter, and that the nature of light is the essential orderer of all things created, he was pointing towards much that is now accepted fact. It was Grosseteste's essentially unitary way of thinking, his rejection of that dualistic mode of thought which broke apart form and content, spiritual and corporeal, the intelligible and the sensible, the theoretical and the empirical, all of which stemmed from the legacy of Greek thought, particularly in its various Aristotelian forms which pervaded mediaeval attitudes, which allowed him to make such profound advances.

The cognisance of objective rationality inherent in the universe as a light-founded and a light-pervaded creation, is the hallmark of Grosseteste's achievement as he looked at the verities of creation in their relation to their Creator. It is a matter of remark that this accomplishment, while not ignored after his death in 1256 (though the paucity of references from the theological circles which might have been expected to take up his work and establish a Grosseteste 'industry' is itself a matter of note) nevertheless unfortunately suffered a neglect of development of his themes in those writers who do refer to him – and, indeed, I would suggest, that the extant text from the works of such persons show little else than superficial acknowledgement of what Grosseteste had accomplished. Little understanding of his thought is apparent – a lack of comprehension on their part.

Several historians claim that there is a neglect of Grosseteste's works and that it is not until the late 14th century and into the 15th that interest in Grosseteste's works becomes evident again.

Richard Dales[1] does not agree with this latter assessment, and in characteristic detailed fashion, with scrupulous textual scholarship, shows that Grosseteste's *Hexaemeron* was extensively used by two important names – Richard Fishacre and Richard Rufus of Cornwall in their respective commentaries on the *Sentences*. But neither of these show any profound understanding (as Dales points out) of Grosseteste's important emphases, and certainly no development of them. Indeed most of their usage of him in lifting parts of his *Hexaemeron* is of inconsequential passages on minor themes. Of his achievement with regard to the nature of light in either the *Hexaemeron* or *De Luce* there is not a word. Indeed, that usage of him is mundane, pedestrian and unimaginative.

It is true that several other figures do quote Grosseteste in their own works, showing at least that reference to his works was still made. D. Sharp, in her work *Franciscan Theology at Oxford in the Thirteenth Century* (Oxford, 1930), attempts to make a case for Grosseteste to be regarded as the founding Father of a Franciscan school of thought, but her argument and her evidence are unconvincing. A. C. Crombie in his *Robert Grosseteste and the Origins of Experimental science, 1100–1700* (Oxford, 1953) attempts to demonstrate an undoubted influence on the thought of his contemporaries, but the evidence for this legacy of Grosseteste is extremely meagre. He instances Roger Bacon, and while it is to be noted that Bacon pirated Grosseteste's works, it has to be said that this was to not very good effect. This criticism, however, in no way detracts from the value of Crombie's work (on which so many have been dependent, acknowledged or not) on Grosseteste himself.

But on the whole it is the surprising lack of a more widespread appreciation and an authoritative attempt to advance his views which is apparent. This whole neglect may be due to several causes. First, that theological endeavour and interest was captivated by the onrush of Thomist theology and the reinterpretation therein of Aristotelian emphases.

Second, that Grosseteste's outspoken criticism of the misuse of high office in Rome had not endeared him to official acknowledgement, affirmation of his works probably suffering. Third, Grosseteste stands out from his contemporaries in his theological methodology and resultant insights, in such a way that the radical difference between his thought and the prevailing modes of working stand out distinctly.

On the other hand, the cautionary observation must be made that argument from extant texts to formulate a decisive theory that Grosseteste had little influence on his near contemporaries, is a dangerous business. What evidences have been instanced, while they do not warrant assumptions that Grosseteste did heavily influence his contemporaries, may well be pointers to a wider but unrecorded, as far as we know, appreciation.

There is a parallel between the fate of Grosseteste's works and thought and that of that sixth century theologian of light, John Philiponos. Philoponos, too, was somewhat under a shadow of disapproval, in that his Trinitarian views were regarded as suspect and that he thereby earned the censure of the church. Indeed, those later than he, who had the timerity to employ his observations, refer to him under the cloak of the anonymous 'the commentator' – usually in reference to his attacks on Aristotle. Aquinas, for example, does just this. His influence was kept simmering for a considerable period, until the west became familiar with him at second-hand, generally through the works of the Arabic commentators who delved deeply into his works and through Simplicius's works which condemn Philoponos's criticisms of Aristotle.

Much underlying the work of Grosseteste on light is found in Philoponos. The created rational order of the universe determined and unified by the nature and quality of light; the relation of that created order to the Uncreated Light which God is; the beginning of that order with the beginning of creation brought into being as a temporal and spatial entity out of nothing (and thereby assigning a beginning to time and space); the beginning not only of the material existence of the universe but of its rational created forms (and thereby destroying any dualistic notion between the external forms of the universe and its corporeal being); light as the purest form of matter moving in strict geometric lines at 'infinite' speed – all these are precepts of Philoponos the significance of which was recognized in whatever literary vehicle they were conveyed to Grosseteste, and taken up, and developed by him.

We may draw out several of these themes pervading the works of such patristic and mediaeval thinkers as a theological perception of the attributes of light and their theological employment.

The first of these which we note in this chapter is the **constancy, regularity,** or **fidelity** of light. The observation that there is a constancy of light moving from an infinitesimal singularity, regularly and straightly diffusing itself on every side, at the beginning, has been noted previously in the text of, and comments on, Grosseteste's *De Luce*. Here, fidelity of light is construed as not only its constant and unique speed, surpassing any other created entity, but its very nature as that which alone can do this. Again, Grosseteste emphasizes this in his comment that only light is capable of such action. In so doing there is implicit – and assumed by him – the fact that the universe is grounded upon a constant which, by its very nature expressed in its action, determines the order and rationality of all created things in their individuality and in their relation one to another, and therefore the rationality and order of the whole. Light is the objective, decisive and rational ground on which all else rests, however, chaotic or unpredictable all else may immediately appear and apparently be. There is an underlying order to which even this disorder refers and to which, in its seemingly bewildering complexity, points.

But in that this constant has a beginning and its activity produces time and space, it is not the Absolute Constant. It can only refer us to that which gave it its beginning and sustains it in its constancy among all created verities.

That attribute of light which is its constancy points us to three interwoven considerations – to the natural order of the universe; to the order which God is in himself as the Uncreated Source of all creation; and to the relation between creation and Creator in terms of the order of double contingency. It is to these and to the attendant view of creation as a creation of light that we now turn.

Richard Dales, in *Viator 9*, 1978, makes the somewhat astonishing statement that the Greek and Latin writers of the fourth and the fifth centuries made the break with ancient patterns of thought regarding nature, and that certain *scattered statements* in the writings of Basil, Gregory of Nyssa, John Damascene, Jerome, and Augustine, *imply at least a de-animation of nature*. He states that these men were interested in other sorts of things (that is, presumably, other than the significance of creation), for though nature for them was regarded as good, it being the handiwork of God, *it did not rank high in their order of priorities; and although the patristic writings contained the seeds of the twelfth century views we are investigating, a new concept of the natural order was not fully and clearly worked out during the patristic period* [2]. These views are that nature *is a self-sufficient, largely mechanical entity*. I would not presume to criticize the scholarship of Dales in all that follows from this opening to his subject, and for what he deduces from the twelfth century writers he goes on to examine. But three points must be made in the face of his patristic observations.

1. The natural order is dealt with sufficiently as a matter of the first importance by the fathers he mentions, Moreover, the omissions even from what he probably intends to be a sample list, are surprizing to say the least, as is his confinement to the fourth century fathers. Irenaeus and Athanasius are quite clear as to the necessity of regarding the natural order in a particular way, as is Origen in his personal approach. The *Hexaemeron* of Basil and that of Ambrose are more than a matter of scattered statements on the subject. There is a clear doctrine of creation in all these patristic thinkers which sets out the question of the significance of the natural order.

2. That nature is *self-sufficient and a mechanical entity* may well be a twelfth century preoccupation with some writers in that period, but it is not the thrust and direction of the patristic age nor of those mediaeval writers who saw the necessity of wrestling with the question of the significance of the order of creation. They establish the dignity, meaning,

worth and purpose of creation and nature, not on a supposed autonomy of nature itself, reading all this out of its face, but in its relation to the Creator. That relation is neither disparaging to nature, nor some sort of primitive view of it, to be equated or paralleled to a 'magical' view of it. If anything, the twelfth century thinkers instanced by Dales were reverting to a type of mythological treatment of nature in trying to elevate a method of supposed understanding of nature out of itself as the final and ultimate ground and truth of all things.

3. The rationality of creation does not depend on its being seen as *self-sufficient and a mechanical entity*. That is to engage in presuppositions and fall into the error of thinking that we can only know what we understand. The belief that we can understand the universe out of itself and finally encompass it around with our explanations is a type of Apollinarianism, for it presupposes that the human mind is the ultimate authority and itself unquestionable. However and with what method these figures instanced by Dales from the twelfth century may have proceeded in their quest of laying bare the natural order, those instanced by Dales and other of their number who made up the patristic period, and indeed Grosseteste and Duns Scotus to mark at least two figures in the later mediaeval period, in differing ways but nevertheless in accord of perception, sought the rationality of nature in that which bestowed rationality, and which therefore is that Rationality beyond creation.

In this way they perceived that there is no constant, imminent, self-sufficient and self-evident, within creation itself to which the rest of nature can be referred. The nature of creation is that of a temporal/spatial entity and therefore with a beginning. It is seen as that which is limited by the very expression of itself as having the disposition of time and space as transient and liable to dissolution. *Here we have no continuing stay* is the common observation underlying the objective reasoning of the patristic period and such of the mediaevalists influenced strongly by the fathers and appreciative of their contribution to understanding creation. What constancy there is in creation is grounded beyond itself in its Source and Upholder.

Nowhere is this dependency more clear than in the patristic and mediaeval treatment of light. In general for these writers the constancy of light lies in its qualitative nearness to the Uncreated Light which God is and as he is witnessed to in scripture. Whatever criticisms may be made of Pseudo-Dionysius, this is his great insight and value of comprehension, that in the final assessment of his work, there is an implicit but strong underlying perception of the double contingency of created light – that it has its own identity as that which is created, but nevertheless utterly depends upon the Uncreated Light which brings it into being for that identity and nature. This is its contingency *from* God, in that it is not God, nor an emanation from him, but has its own created nature and dimension, and its contingency *to* God in that its dependence upon him for its inception and its nature is the ground of its own identity for what it is in itself.

Created light, according to Pseudo-Dionysius, *is an image* of Him who is the Good. The goodness of God reaches from the highest to the lowliest of all beings, yet is transcendent over all created things. The goodness of God expresses itself by giving light to every created thing. That light is therefore the image of that divine benevolence. The sun, which constantly pours forth its light, is such an image. The idea of the constancy of created light is present in Pseudo-Dionysius's thoughts here, for, as he makes clear, the light of the sun is universal, and if anything fails to receive that light, the defect lies not with light but with that which should receive its pervasive and generous action.

Pseudo-Dionysius[3] lists three aspects of the demeanour of light in its constancy, these being: 1. the universality of light, its all-pervasiveness, typified by the light of the sun. Nothing is hidden from its rays which it extends in abundance. It is the source of all life, the sustainer of growth, the ever-renewable development to perfection and the fulfilment of all things; 2. it is the author of time, this time which we experience and which typifies all created things; 3. he brings this all together in speaking of that which light signifies, the goodness of God which recapitulates all creation, returning all to itself. That goodness, of which light is the created and active image, is the constant of all creation.

> The Good brings back all things to itself, for it is the divine
> Source and unifier of the total entirety of all things. Each exis-
> tence looks to it as [its] source, as that which holds all
> together, and as [its] fulfilment.[4]

There then follows an observation on the yearning of all
things for and towards that Good, for, as the argument runs,
there is a basic, instinctive and intuitive recognition in every
rational entity that its existence depends upon that Good as
its beginning, continuance and end. This applies not only to
rational thinking beings, but to the natural condition of even
inanimate created things, which in their own way, demonstrate the dependency of what they are on that Good.

> Thus it is with regard to light, the visible image of the Good.
> It compels and brings back all things to itself.

The originative and recapitulative nature and action of light
is emphasised by Pseudo-Dionysius with regard to created
entities and all creation in its totality. Light is as the sun, the
rays of which are the common constant throughout the
world. Moreover, this is not a matter of physical light only,
but the very presence and activity of light illuminates the
mind. That which is made manifest by the light is appreciated as such by the mind. It allows us to see and in seeing to
understand. In other words it not only is order but the
means, by that very order made manifest, of appreciating
order, beauty and harmony.

> ... the Good which is above all light is given the name 'light of
> the mind' ... it fills every mind above and transcending the
> world both around it and within it, with its light.[5]

This Goodness, by its light of which created light is the
image, persuades thinking beings of the rationality of all that
it has created, for it refers them, by enlightening all creation
and illuminating their minds, to that which lies beyond creation, namely itself, as the Rationality which bestows created
rationality.

One of the extensions of the Good as light is the conse-
quent attribute of 'beauty'. Here too, we find a constancy.
Beauty, as an attribute of the divine Goodness, bestows
corresponding beauty on created things according to their

nature and place and function. Like the recapitulative nature and action of light, it calls and gathers all things to itself. But its significance, and its ability to do this, consists in the fact that it is the Beauty that is beyond all things. The beauty of created things is an image pointing to that divine Beauty.

This Beauty, as with light, remains constant to itself. It has its unassailed and unassailable integrity.

It is always so, equably, inalterably so.[6]

It is not subject to time's sway or to displacement, though it may be regarded as beautiful to one thing and not to another. That, however, is not a comment on any supposed change-ableness in it, for there is not any such, but a recognition of the arbitrariness of the sensibility of created things.

It may be added that Pseudo-Dionysius characteristically takes the opportunity to remark on *nonbeing* in his discussion on beauty and created existences. This is significant, for he construes *nonbeing*, that is 'nothingness', as being in relation to God. It has no right of existence; it is not existence; it (and it is not even 'it') can only be perceived within the context of that which Is – in the first instance, God, and in the second, that which God brings into existence out of non-existence. It becomes in fact a beautiful and good concept *when applied transcendently to God*.[7] I construe Pseudo-Dionysius to mean here that the concept *nonbeing* serves to enhance the fact that only God exists as beauty, goodness, light, and that all created things have their existence only from him. The concept points away from its non-self by its very negation, just as positive images point away from themselves in their positive appropriateness in their created limitations, to God and his attributes.

I would further suggest that, by this device and perception, he utterly denies any dualism, for all that is must, by virtue of being, be caused by, participate in and find its fulfilment in the Goodness, Light and Beauty which God is. The goodness of existence is affirmed, and no room is left for any dependence of created things on chaos, darkness and a supposed positive force of that which is the antithesis of God. The negation of existence can only witness to existence.

That Beauty which God is holds everything in its totality

and its diversity in a harmonious whole. There is in *The Divine Names* 704BC a most moving passage as to the unity and yet diversity of all created things, from the highest hierarchical existence and function of the angelic host through the ranks of creation, in which the

> harmony and love between them do not abolish identity.

Creation is regarded as a single entity, the glory of which is its unity in magnificent diversity – a diversity and unity to be seen and understood by reference to the Goodness, Light and Beauty of the transcendent Creator, to whom and from whom that unity and diversity is contingent and to whom they point in the light, beauty and goodness of their created status corresponding in that dimension to the God who ineffably transcends them as their source, sustainer and fulfilment.

The constancy of light depends on light's contingent relation with, and creaturely correspondence to, that Uncreated Light. The distinction between created light and the Uncreated Light which God is is underlined in Grosseteste's *Commentary on the Celestial Hierarchies*. In his fifteenth chapter of that commentary, he explores and develops Pseudo-Dionysius's use of symbols as applied to God and to angels, the purest and most 'spiritual' of created beings. Images and symbols to describe God and the angels are discussed in terms of their propriety judged against that to which they are applied. As a symbol, nothing created is really appropriate when applied to God, for the qualitative distinction between Creator and creature will not permit such a facile transference. When applied to angels, who after all are created beings, the purity of their existences will not permit the application of gross, material things as symbols to describe them.

What Grosseteste is labouring here is the very important principle that all symbolic language taken from the created entities and existences in which we live and move and have our being, has to be emptied of its creaturely content if it is applied to God. If applied to angels, then the same process, though qualified, has to be undertaken. For while some symbols (such as light) are appropriate for a description of the angelic state, light being the purest form of matter, as the angels are, the more earthly images are not, unless they too be discharged from their normal material and corporeal associations. The great danger in the application of symbolic language to God and the angels is that if that process does not undergo the mental discipline of purging creaturely content and connotation, then an anthropomorphic deity and a humanoid heavenly host will be conjectured. In this, the distinction between Creator and creature and higher and lower orders of creation will be blurred and disappear.

But Grosseteste, in the course of his commentary here, points out that it is easy enough to see this danger when we are operating with corporeal images. That they are *unlike symbols* is manifest and the danger evident. The real danger lies in the unthinking and untutored application of immaterial symbols such as light and the heavens, for the mind is less able to purge even the purest of these of its creaturely content in this application.

Light falls with this category. It is the most alluring of images in speaking about God, yet, it must be borne in mind that it is created. It is not an extension of Uncreated light, an emanation of the divine. It utterly depends on the divine Light for its existence. Constancy is the attribute only of the divine Light. The constancy of created light is that it is that by which God determines that creation is characterized, for it is the best created correspondent to his divine existence.

We may conclude that the constancy of light is its contingent relation to and from God. That relation determines the character of creation as a creation of light and therefore of rationality and order, beauty and harmony, and unity, corresponding in its created dimension to the uncreated Order and Perfection, Rationality and Concord, and Unity which God is as Father, Son and Holy Spirit.

The constant self-propagation of light does not mean that light is self-sufficient and autonomous. Its constancy, and all that stems from that as the nature of light in its utter rationality, is a matter not of nature but of grace. Therein is the foundation and sustenance of that created constancy. Grosseteste, throughout his works, does not make the distinction of the 'Schoolmen' between nature and grace. All creation is grace. That is its nature. That is the constancy of light.

As a created universal constant, light is a fitting symbol of God's constancy. But as a symbol it points beyond its creaturely status to that which no earthly image can encompass.

Theology is obliged to take heed of the fact that from James Clerk Maxwell onwards, and past Einstein, all that has been and is unfolded in the scientific disciplines only enhances all theological endeavour in perceiving the propriety of light not only as a symbol of God, but as an 'earnest' (in the biblical sense) of God's constancy as he is *in se*, existing as the eternal and undivided Trinity, the Father and the Son bound in the bond of constant divine love, the Holy Spirit, and as he is *ad extra* in the expression of his Being towards creation in constant love. God is as he acts, and acts as he is, constant and unchanging, not in the sense of rigid, mechanical existence, but in the quality of his existence as an existence of love within his Triune being and love towards that which he has created. The constancy of God is the unvarying and unreserved love of God.

This is why the expression of that love towards creation, the incarnation, God's staking his own being on his creation, is spoken of in terms of light. The prologue of St John's Gospel, and all the references to our Lord thereafter in terms of light, has to do with that constancy. If light has, in Einstein's words, *a unique metaphysical status in the universe*, that is but a pointer to the unique status in the midst of his own handiwork of the one of whom it is self-declared *I am the light of the world*, and of whom it is witnessed that he is the *true Light which lighteth every man that cometh into the world. He was in the world and the world was made by him* ...

The constancy of the speed of light irrespective of whether its source is moving or static and without regard to the physical disposition of its observer, whether moving in any direction or static, points to the unqualified constancy of the God who has created all things by that Word made flesh, and bestows graciously and without measure, his grace which is that Jesus Christ on whom all life and light depends, without privilege, favour or discrimination as to worth, establishing existences as he will in a diversity of equality to the created order. The trustworthiness of light, as the constant of all creation, to which all things and the time and space of all things, are referred in order to understand them, is, within the created dimension, in whatever circumstances, the appropriate symbol of the constant faithfulness of God on which all faith, life and light, rests, and from which they spring.

5

The Unity and Diversity of Created Light and the Nature of God

THE SECOND attribute of light to which we now turn for consideration is its property concerning both **unity** and **diversity**. Light has a unique place amongst all the created entities; it is not only the first of these but the determiner, disposer and orderer of them. All else depends on light. Every object is what it is in itself and what it is in relation to all others because of light. Not only is there a rational harmony in the co-existence of all created entities formed, undergirded and embraced by light, but there is a fundamental bond forged by light between physical reality and the mental capacity to comprehend that reality – between what is known and the process of knowing, a sapient cohesion between intelligibility and intelligence.

Above all, there is the theological claim, expressed variously through the ages, that light is the created correspondence of the uncreated Rationality which God is in himself as he exists as the Triune God, Father and Son bound in the bond of divine love, the Holy Spirit. Created light has been seen by theologians – Irenaeus, Athanasius, Basil, John Philoponos, Pseudo-Dionysius and Robert Grosseteste, to instance but a few who have perceived the importance and fundamental role of light – as therefore holding a determinative place in the relation between Creator and creation as the creaturely reflection, the created expression, of the will and purpose of uncreated Light.

Light not only characterizes the rationality of creation and the rationality of the mind, but refers all created existence and activity, in the rational, recapitulative relation it has bestowed upon it in that existence and activity's own dimension, to the Rationality of the uncreated Light which God is. Light, out of its essential and primordial simplicity and constant activity, both qualifies creation as that which is ordered in the rich diversity of its unity, and the harmonious unity of its diversity, as distinct from the Creator in the integrity of its created rationality, and brings that unity and diversity into the context of the intelligible ground of all, the Rationality of God, the uncreated Light of the Creator.

Central to this priority of the place of created light accorded it by theology, is the incarnation. The taking by the Creator Word of God of the created realities to himself in becoming man, flesh of our flesh, blood of our blood, bone of our bone, mind of our mind, without compromizing, changing or forsaking his Godness, or denying the factuality of our estate in all its frailty and mortality, is construed in a long line of theological thinking flowing from its evangelical fount, St John's Gospel, in terms of light. The incarnation is interpreted particularly as the action of him who is God from God, one with the Father and the Spirit, bringing to bear his Person, as the Light of Light by whom all things without exclusion were made (and who enlightens everyone who comes into the world, which light is the life of humanity), into the midst of the created realities, grasping them in union with himself. Uncreated Light, the Beginning and the End, the Author and Perfecter of all, has his place in his own creation. Indeed, he has declared creation, all time and space which is the existence of all created things, to be his place.

Here the relation of Creator and creature is expressed as inseparable but unconfused union, and as the grounding of all created existence, characterized by created light, in the existence of him who is uncreated Light. 'He who dwells in light unapproachable' has approached, or, in Irenaean terms, 'the Invisible has become visible', 'the Incomprehensible, comprehensible'. He gives himself to his creation, but does not give himself up in the sense that he ceases to be Creator Lord over all, Invisible, Incomprehensible. Uncreated Light reveals himself in the actualities and agency of created light so that created realities in their limitations and dimension which characterize them as created, are not swallowed up but affirmed in their relation to him. Nor is the creaturely mind overwhelmed, but established and directed in the operation of created light pointing to that uncreated Light in that light's correspondence to, and relation with, him.

By the incarnation the principle of double contingency is thrown up in sharp relief. This is not to say that the incarnation is a general statement of such. The relation of the human to the divine in the incarnation is unique in that it is the act and event of the divine taking human nature into personal, inseparable but unconfused union with himself. The relation of the creation to which the Word came, to the Creator depends not on a union with the divine, but on a *community of union*, as Irenaeus expressed it, of creation with God made man, with the Word made flesh, with this Jesus Christ. The relation of creature to Creator is Christocentric, and as such is seen as a relation first of dependence for its beginning, sustaining and fulfilling – creation's contingency *to* God; second of its distinction as that which is created with its own dimension, nature, quality and identity bestowed by the Creator as the rational creaturely correspondence to his uncreated Rationality – its contingency *from* God. Contingency *to* and contingency *from* are held in perfect harmony in the *community of union* of creation with Christ, and therefore with the divine existence. Here in Christ, there is found the affirmation of the creature as it is in itself which integrity it can only be and have in its relation to the Creator, in whose Rationality its rationality is affirmed and established.

The incarnation is the personal presence of the Creator as one of his own creatures amidst the realities of the created dimension. As such, and only as such, is it the revelation of God, for the incarnation does not mean that this Jesus Christ, the Word made flesh, is merely something about God, or something of God, or a reflection of God, or that he is only a witness to an invisible Light which he is not in himself. It does mean that he is that creative Light of God, incarnate, the personal embodiment of uncreated Light in the midst of the actualities of creation. Revelation, therefore, is more than admission to objective knowledge of God. It is this – but only because the knowledge of God which we are so given is essentially the permission and granting of our sharing, our participation in, the knowledge which God has of himself as he exists as the Triune God, Father and Son bound in the bond of divine love, the Holy Spirit. Thus it is that *in thy light we see light.*[1]

Only in the context of the Rational Order of the divine Existence can we see the panorama of the realities of creation in all the significance of their unity and diversity. This last statement may be thought to be, or bordering on, what is sometimes called 'ontologism'. The question of ontology, of the relation of created truth to divine Truth, and of the knowing human mind to the divine Mind, will be considered below when we look at the supposed 'exemplarism' of Grosseteste. Suffice it for the moment to say that the above statement is not to be read as indicating even a semblance of what ontologism implies.

In this perception, light exercises the fundamental and determinative role. The various theologians listed above are, I would suggest, uniform in their insistence on this, which further rests on their cognisance of the relation of created light to uncreated Light, expressed in their individual ways.

Pseudo-Dionysius[2] dwells on the nature, action and para-deigmatic role of light. He does so in terms of archetypes and their images.

> Light comes from the Good, and light is the image of this archetypal Good. In this way the Good is also praised by the name 'Light', just as an archetype is revealed in its image.

The goodness of God, who is transcendent over all else, pervades everything from the highest existence to the lowest, yet remains transcendent. This goodness bestows light, creating, enlivening, preserving and perfecting all things which look to it for *measure, eternity, number, order* – that is to say, for identity and purpose. It is the beginning and end of the universe, and the power which embraces it. Every single thing without exception can share and enjoy the benefits of light; if certain things do not, then the fault lies not in the unstinting generosity of light, but in these things themselves. It is the apportioner of hours, days and all time, and is itself their measure. The Good is the source of all things and reca-pitulates them in calling them back to it as their source and fulfilment. All things yearn for it and to perceive it, even, in their own way, inanimate objects. This same thought was later to be expressed by John Calvin, who remarks that every element in creation cries out for its eventual resurrection in Christ (Calvin: *Commentary on the Epistle to the Romans*).

Light as the visible image of this Good reflects its action and liberality, nurturing and gathering together all things. It is the cause and upholder both of the various identities of created entities and of their recapitulative unity in itself.

Physical light is related to what is called 'the light of the mind', for just as created light is the providential creature of the Good in giving existence and order, so too the Good imparts the light of knowledge of itself to all sentient beings, super-celestial or within the world, allowing them, by gathering them together in unity of mind, out of their diverse and opposing notions into *a single, pure, coherent and true knowledge*, to perceive the objective truth of what is reality itself.

It is in much the same vein that John Philiponos describes and expounds light. He sees the universe qualified as a creation of light, light begun, light filled, light whole and entire and final. He does so not in terms of light as the image of an archetype, but as that which is given its own integrity as it is in itself, and, as that prime and definitive and concluding factor of all creation, distinct from uncreated Light and neither an extension or a shadow of it.

Despite the fact that he is generally regarded as a Neoplatonist Christian, or even a Christian Neoplatonist, Philiponos certainly rejected the dualism within the totality of creation inherent in both Neoplatonism and Aristotelianism, and built on that emphasis found in the teaching particularly of Irenaeus, Athanasius, Basil and Cyril of Alexandria, making a decisive differentiation between Creator and creation which latter he construed as the totality of all that is and which is not the Creator, whether of heavenly or earthly existence. But that clear distinction opened up for him an appreciation of the relation between the Creator and creation which he saw clearly in terms of double contingency.

Out of this came his pioneering physics of light, which long before Grosseteste (who indeed is undoubtedly dependent on him, if not from actual texts of Philoponos, but probably via books of patristic proof texts which did not name their sources, or through the Arabic commentators who certainly knew the works of Philoponos, and through the writings of Simplicius) advanced the idea that created light, from its inception in the uncreated Light of God, dispersed itself, giving energy and ordering the universe.

According to Philoponos, light travels in straight lines at an infinite speed, permeating the whole universe it has ordered. For him, the universe is to be regarded as a creation of light under the creative and preserving power of God's uncreated Light. While God indeed 'dwells in light unapproachable', he is yet the Source and Sustainer of all light and enlightenment within the created order. The parallels of Grosseteste's thought with the earlier theologian are obvious.

Philoponos brought his physics and theology together in applying analogies taken from the nature, quality and behaviour of light to the doctrine of the incarnation of the Word, the uncreated Light of God amid the light-determined created dimension as man, and interprets the doctrine of creation in terms of the Creator as Light, and creation as light contingent to and from that self-same uncreated Light made flesh. Knowledge and knowing, too, are a matter of double contingency, where the light of human rationality has this relation to the Rationality which God is, and is able to perceive the intelligibilities of all that is created in the light of creation's relation of the Creator in and by and through the Word made flesh.

Such was Philoponos's insistence on the relation between creature and Creator that his doctrine of the incarnation, in which this relation is personally fulfilled in the assumption of the flesh by the Word, was suspected of being infected with monophysitism. This is unjust, and the result of a misreading of what double contingency means – in this case to the ignoring of the stress on the integrity of that which is created, the contingency *from*, and the exaggerated interpretation of Philoponos's detractors of the contingency to, which, thus isolated, can be construed in the last resort as suggesting the concurrence of the Creator with his creatures and his creatures with him.

The works of John Philoponos were regarded therefore with disfavour, and fell into ((as far as we know) relative obscurity for a time. That copies were retained and circulated (but to what extent we do not know) is clear, however, for his achievements and his observations on light were later taken up by the Arabic commentators either passingly or to greater extent – Averroes, Avicebrol, Avicenna, for example, but particularly by Alghazali – and hence passed to the attention of some western theologians to greater or lesser extent. The parallels with, and indeed the usage of close terminology to, Philiponos by Grosseteste, suggests that the former's influence was more important by the thirteenth century (and perhaps since the 11th century) than has been recognized.

Grosseteste developed the same imagery of light employed by Philoponos in his individual way. That light should have this status of corresponding most closely to the uncreated Light which God is, exercising by this dignity a central unifying and diversifying role in creation, pointing all things in the recapitulative relation it bestows amongst them and upon them, to that uncreated Light and Rationality which brought it and them into being out of nothing, made it eminently suitable as a source of appropriate imagery for the bond between Creator and creation as a totality in all its ordered and harmonious diversity. It is the foundation of all things, binding them in their respective identities in mutual harmony and all with God:

> Quapropter Deus, qui lux est, ab ipsa luce cuius tanta est dignitas merito inchoavit sex dierum opera.[3]
> Wherefore, God who is light, by that selfsame light which assuredly is the dignity of all things, laid the foundation of the six days' work.

Illustrations taken from light by Grosseteste in his awareness of its status and role, are not to be thought of as an indulging in what is called 'natural theology'. There is, of course, a place for natural theology, and that is within the framework of God's Self-revelation, where the verities of creation are seen in their proper context in the light of the Creator and his Self-knowledge. It is within that context that Grosseteste employs his light imagery.

The real bond between God and his creation, the intelligibility of that, and the resultant developing knowledge (in this case concerning the mode of the transmission of knowledge) to be gained from it, is instanced by this example of his appealing to the activity of light with regard to an object and the subject observing it, pointing to the Trinity.

> *Hec itaque tria Trinitatis exampla est invenire universaliter in omnibus. Inter res autem corporeas manifestissimum Trinitatis exemplum est ignis, sive lux, que necessario de se gignit splendorem; et hec duo in se reflectunt mutuum fervorem. In coniunctione autem corporei cum incorporeo, prima exampla sunt in formis sensibilibus, et speciebus formarum sensibilium generatis in sensibus, et intentione animi coniungente speciem genita in sensu cum forma gignente que est extra sensum. Et huius rei evidentior est examplacio in visu. Color enim rei colorate gignit de se speciem sibi similem in oculo videntis; et intencio animi videntis coniungit speciem coloris genitam in oculo cum colore gingnente exterius; et sic unit gignens et genitum quod apprehensio visus non distinguit inter speciem genitam et colorem gignentem; fitque una visio ex gignente et genito et intencione copulante genitum cum gignente. Et similiter est ista trinitas in quolibet exteriorem sensuum.*[4]

Thus therefore there are three examples of the Trinity to be found universally in everything. Amongst bodily things the most manifest example of the Trinity is fire, or light, which by necessity begets splendour from itself, and these two reflect their mutual warmth. However, in the conjunction of the bodily with the incorporeal, the prime examples are in forms apprehended by the senses and in species of sensible forms generated in the senses, and by the intent of the mind the species begotten in the sense is yoked with the begetting form which is outside the sense. However, the most evident example of these things is in the sight. For the colour of a thing begets as coloured the species similar to itself in the eye of the beholder; and the intention of the viewing mind conjoins the species begotten of colour in the eye with the external begetting colour; and thus begetter unites with begotten, because the apprehension of the sight does not distinguish between the begotten species and the begetting colour; and there is made one vision out of the begotten by the deliberate embrace of the begetter with the begotten. And this Trinity is similar in any exterior sense.

This argument is an analogy to the Trinity of the Father (the begetter), the Son (the begotten) and the Holy Spirit (who binds them in the embrace of divine love). The illustration is that of the threefold nature of perception centred on the operation of light whereby the external object with its quality of colour and the internal, mental image are joined as one by the informing activity of light. The mode and result of perception is a process of light which in itself is analogous to that uncreated Light which God is.

For Grosseteste there was but one field of knowledge, all aspects of creation in the unity of its diversity and the diversity of its unity, profoundly bracketed together with the Creator by light which is centred on the Word made flesh, the Self-revelation of God, whereby uncreated Light is present to the realities and verities of his own handiwork. With regard to all created being and knowing, the cohesive factor, concentrated on the incarnation, is light, which is seen in its diversity as physical light and as the intelligible light of the human mind, and in the unity of its operation of both lightening and enlightening, as that which is created directly by the uncreated, intelligible Light of God to which it most closely, above all other created entities, corresponds. Light is the recapitulator of all its results, and it does so by shedding upon all things the knowledge of that uncreated Light which has grasped his own handiwork to himself in the incarnation, and pointing them to their ultimate truth, significance and purpose in that uncreated Light.

Whenever it is stated, however, that the truth of each thing in creation can only be seen in the context of the Light of the Creator, a suspicion of ontologism is raised. Ontologism is that which claims that the mind is qualified to gain and grasp knowledge only by way of direct participation in the mind of God. This idea has been further strengthened, though not necessarily deliberately so, by some commentators who perceive in Grosseteste's works a methodological exemplarism in his use of imagery. This is closely linked to the claim that Grosseteste operated with a 'metaphysic of light' (e.g. J. McEvoy: *The Philosophy of Robert Grosseteste*, in passim). Exemplarism can walk hand in hand with ontologism, and indeed with metaphysic of archetypes and images, for it consists of the idea that the truth of every created object lies in the conformity of that object to its exemplar, that is its ideal or standard, in the divine mind or creative Word of God.

Both exemplarism and ontologism are found in the thought of Augustine who operated with a basic dualism between the intelligible and the sensible realms. It is necessary to remember that a distinction between Creator and creature, the spiritual and the corporeal, is not a dualistic separation. The teaching particularly of Irenaeus and Athanasius makes this distinction, speaking of God, out of Isaiah's biblical emphasis, as the God 'who is beyond comparison'; but they do not make a separation between Creator and creature, as though God were the prisoner of his own eternity and unable to have converse and concourse towards and with and in his own creation. The unfortunate direction which the positing of such a gulf between Creator and creature, the eternal and the temporal, takes is that God is regarded inevitably as being wordless.

The hint of this is found in Augustine who, with framework of dualism between the intelligible and sensible realms and his pyschologizing of Christian belief and awareness, distinguishes between the senses of sight and sound which in the sensible realm are physically separated, and the intelligible realm, inward consciousness, so that in the realm of the intelligible (and this applies in his thought not only to the life of God, but to the human inward mental perception and consciousness also) word and light co-alesce. Now, of course, in the incarnation the Word and Light of God are acknowledged as identical but for Augustine this meant that 'God speaks to us by illuminating us', that is, that the Word of God towards us is in the last resort the shining of God's eternal Light and our sharing in it through 'reflections conceived in the soul by divine Light'. This develops into a view that word is transformed solely into light, both for the Word of God and for the substance of faith, and our contact with God through his Word becomes a matter of illumination, with all the mysticism that that eventually involves. Thus, ultimately, the sensible realm of our temporal/spatial existence is disparaged, and the real truth about created entities found only in their intelligible exemplars.

As T. F. Torrance points out[5]:

> The difficulty became greater, not less, when Augustinian theology with its other-worldly spirituality was recast in abstractive Aristotelian terms, when the separation between the temporal and the eternal, the world and God, took on a harder form. On the one hand, the notion of God as the unmoved Mover seriously damaged the understanding of divine interaction with the empirical world. 'God does not become anything', as Peter Lombard expressed it – a conception of divine inertia which introduced lasting problems into the doctrines of the incarnation and the real presence. The shining of the divine Light across the gap between God and the world was more conceivable than the actual coming of a Word which eternally inheres in the unchanging Being of God. On the other hand, the intellectualist notion of word as formed by the intellect in its union with the object to be the vehicle of clear-cut concepts derived through the reason, reinforced the need for contemplation which strives for illumination beyond the grasp of reason and which rises above the level of words and concepts to reach the spiritual content and reality that transcends them. Hence we find a very important place being given to a form of Neoplatonic and Pseudo-Dionysian 'apophaticism' in which the human spirit 'tails-off', as it were, in a wordless and conceptless mystical vision of God.

If light is divorced from 'word', that is, from the rational existence and expression of that existence (and this applies to God as well as humanity), then it can only be thought of as either a substitute for the rational identity of the being, or as only obliquely related to it. In the first case, a false unity which means the eventual mingling together in promiscuous anonymity causes a confusion of a 'oneness' of all created existences with an amorphous and indistinguishable One. In the second, no related light-order of existences, with the purposeful identity of their light-determined integrities upheld in their relation to each other, can be acknowledged, the Trinity becomes a Tritheistic concept, the construction of creation construed as a collection of disparate entities where tragic individualism is rife, and for both God and the created dimension, artificially mechanical concepts of expressing the order of existence are posited.

In the first, knowledge of God is so 'spiritualized' and 'mysticized' that the human mind and the divine Mind are indistinguishable; in the second, the knowledge of God can only be through institutional means and hard and fast concepts. The first is confusion, the second separation. But, as in every such case of opposite attitudes, the first can lead to separation in the still present necessity of ordering human existence which it does so mechanically as a means to a 'spiritual' end, an artificially pragmatic ordering which is attended by the divorce of rationality, and, indeed, practical morality, from what is deemed to be 'spirituality'. The second can lead to the eventual confusion in the divinization of its institutions and concepts.

It is in this context of the necessity of appreciating the role of light with regard to the respective rational integrities of both God and humanity in their distinction and relation, that exemplarism and ontologism should be seen.

The interpretation of Grosseteste's theological method highlights the question of exemplarism stemming from Augustine. I would dispute the assertion by McEvoy (one contention which is certainly not meant to question the depths of his scholarship or to disparage his significant contribution to an understanding of Grosseteste's thought) regarding Grosseteste's procedure and his use of exemplarism, namely that[6]

> a favourite doctrine of his, and one to which he returns at every opportunity and in all his works. Each created reality has a truth which consists in its conformity to its eternal exemplar in the divine mind or creative word of God ... It follows logically that the mind can only claim possession of complete truth concerning any individual thing when it can see, not only the object itself, but the exemplar which is its standard (rectitudo, regula). In other words, created truth can be seen only in the supreme truth, the light of whose eternal reason must be present to the beholder and to the objects ('as Augustine says').

I contend this on several grounds. First, within the text here being examined by McEvoy, and, indeed, as McEvoy himself acknowledges, Grosseteste asserts the reality of finite truth. This surely at least begins to safeguard the integrity of the created entities in their own verities. Supreme truth is not to be likened to the light of the sun, which, in its resplendence, unequalled by any other lights, overpowers them by its light. Rather it is as the action of the sun on colours – the sum shining upon objects to reveal them as they are in themselves.

It seems to me by this very observation, that Grosseteste is affirming that created entities do possess their own integrity and that what is required is a broader illumination to perceive just that – not a referring of them to their hypothetical ideals in the divine mind or the heavenly dimension where their real truth lies, and they but a shadow of that.

Second, it is the source of that further illumination which is important over against the notion of exemplarism. Here I would wish to argue that for Grosseteste's theology, there is a methodology which over-rules exemplarism as the determinative of his outlook. That source is the Word who is the Light of God – that is, the Light of God as Word. Grosseteste never presumes to deal with the Word as he is in himself in the internal and eternal relations of the Trinity. He firmly anchors knowledge on the Word made flesh – that is, on the affirmation by God of the created dimension in taking it to himself at the incarnation. It is this which colours his *De Cessatione Legalium*, for example.

The incarnation for Grosseteste is not some divine afterthought to deal with the sin of humanity after that appeared. Rather, as I have suggested in *The Anachronism of Time*, Grosseteste's tentative thought is that the incarnation is the reason for creation, that is, the purpose of creation is that it should be that which is not God, but embraced by, loved by, and united to, God, in its own identity for what it is in itself. In any case, Grosseteste is clear that the incarnate Word is the subject matter and endeavour of *that most sacred wisdom which is called theology*. In the Word made flesh, the creation is affirmed for what it is as the handiwork of God, and not referred to some supposed higher truth about itself.

Third, the whole question of what the 'deification' of humanity means is pertinent here as an example of this. 'Deification' for Grosseteste does not mean that our humanity is swallowed up in the divine Life and we are seen to be

not what we were, but rather, that humanity is given, by the
Word made flesh, participation in the divine Life, precisely as
humanity, and in that participation finds its establishment in
its double contingency as humanity to and from God.

Fourth, we cannot avoid Grosseteste's insistence that there
must be a unifying principle for all creation. That unity is
expressed not in terms of reference to what creation supposedly truly is in an ideal in the mind of God, but to what it
actually is in the Word made flesh – not in the Word in isolation from the flesh. Light is that which binds us to the Word
as the uncreated Light of God in the flesh, to whom it bears
witness in the correspondence of its created dimension to
that uncreated Light. The unifying, and therefore the rational, ordering principle, which binds the universe together in
all its diversity is this Word made flesh. God himself, being
other than creation, and, as Creator not of, or identified
with, the created dimension, cannot be within the universe as
its unifying principle. He is transcendent. Man, as the micro-
cosm (in Grosseteste's view), possessing the four elements
which make up the universe in his existence, could be such a
principle, yet neither collectively nor individually, can he
fully be. He is within and not more than the creation. For the
unifying principle to be effectively such, it must be both of
and more than the universe. Only the union between God
and humanity could be such. Hence the incarnation.

Uncreated Light as the Word thus brings itself to bear on
all creation with respect to, and unity with, creation in the
assumption of human flesh and nature. Christ is, in his
humanity in its union with the Word, what no other man can
be – the unifying principle of creation.

In *De Veritate*, Grosseteste discusses the relation of truths
to the ultimate truth, using Augustine and Anselm as his
authorities, and apparently using the language of exemplarism. We have to remember, however, that this work is but
part, and an early part, of his theological development. It is
further to be held in mind, as Grosseteste was surely aware,
that there is a difference between Anselm and Augustine in
the question of knowledge. This refers to what has been
mentioned above, namely Augustine's particular theology of
illumination, and the danger inherent in this that knowledge

becomes a matter of attempting to escape from the bounds of created existence with the attendant loss of created identity and the merely oblique or allegorical regard for created objects as exemplarism assists us to the mystical heights.

Behind this lay Augustine's emphasis on the Word as ultimately, solely the Light of God. Anselm countered this by insisting that behind all our understanding both of the verities of created entities and God's revelation through Scripture bearing witness to the Word made flesh, we must appreciate that there is *intima locutio apud Summam Substantiam* – speech lodged in the very heart of God's existence. The knowledge of God in his Self-revelation is a matter of God communicating his very Self in his Word, that Word which exists with the Father and the Spirit in the internal and eternal Being of God. The Rationality of God confronts us in adapting to our limitations, without ceasing to be that Rationality. It is in the midst of the realities and intelligibilities of the created order that the Word which does not cease to inhere in the Being of God makes his place, and affirms his creation. That place and that affirmation is where faith, with its rationality of the creature corresponding to the Rationality of the Word, is evoked. The light of being and the light of understanding is firmly affixed to the Word made flesh as the Light of God as Word.

Behind Anselm's emphasis lies a pronounced κατα φυσιν mode of thought – an objective way of thinking in which the mind allows itself to be informed by the integrity of the object confronting it. This, I would suggest, lies also behind Grosseteste's theological thinking. Anselm as much as Augustine is one of his authorities.

If exemplarism seems to be present in his works, the claim that it is a basic method for his thinking needs to be reappraised. In the instance of *De Veritate*, this work falls, in any case, in his formative years as a theologian, and the further note may be made that the use of Augustine's emphases was one expected of thinkers in theology of the period in the west. Neglect to do so would render the work and the author suspect of disregard for accepted authority.

Certainly ontologism which sometimes lies behind exemplarism, is not to be laid at Grosseteste's door, as McEvoy does point out (*The Philosophy of Robert Grosseteste*, p. 326). That supreme or divine light requires to be shed on both thinking subject and perceived object, if the former is to be appreciated the full truth of the latter lying in its exemplar in the divine Mind, is one claim of exemplarism. The extension of this is that the thinking subject has to be privy to the divine Mind. That some have been so is noted by Grosseteste in *De Veritate*, but the very paucity of his examples (Moses and Paul biblically, and extended also to include the Blessed Virgin), the fact that these intimate contacts with the divine Mind have been momentary, exceptional rather than general, for particular rather than for inclusive reasons, rules out such experiences as the norm of knowledge. In any case, Grosseteste is not dogmatic about these examples; he is even hesitant in bringing them to note. Moreover, he states that all human beings have the divine light (a comment, surely, on the action of God towards the creature rather than the creature rising towards God), though some do not recognize it for what it is or whence it comes, being like those who enjoy the daily light but, as the weakness of the eye does not permit us to look at the sun, cannot perceive its source. Others do so recognize that the presence of this light must be divine, while yet others, the pure in heart and mind, see the light of Truth for what it is in itself. In so stating, Grosseteste is describing the normal human condition regarding knowledge. He sharply distinguishes these categories of knowing persons from those very few to whom the beatific vision has been granted. The inordinate illuminationism which is ontologism is not a characteristic of Grosseteste's thought.

It may be recognized that in ontologism there lurks an Apollinarian tendency – in that the mind which seeks to penetrate the divine Mind and lose itself there, regards itself to be in no need of humility before, reformation in accordance with, and adjustment to, the objective verities, which, as they are in themselves, are but little moment to it, but can only regard itself as 'unfallen' and capable of achieving the heights of divinity. It essentially advocates the replacement of the human mind with the divine Mind.

In the case of exemplarism in Grosseteste's thought, that, I would propose, is a more of a convenient because conventional, and, at the time of his theological development, a limited, vehicle, for his observations about knowledge. His Christocentricity with his treatment of light, its nature, quality, role and operation, centred on the uncreated Light of God as the Word made flesh, and leading to a view of the double contingency of a creation so held in its unity and diversity, over-rules an exemplarism which is supposedly central to and determinative of his thought. To claim such a centrality is a case of not being able to see the theological wood for the philosophical trees.

Sir Richard Southern, with characteristic, straightforward perception in analysis and interpretation of his subjects, has noted with regard to Grosseteste:

> I have ... mentioned the scientific grounds for his concentration on light – its universality and its strict conformity with the rules of geometry in its behaviour. When he turned to theology, he found equally compelling indications of the fundamental role of light. Commentators on this feature of his thought often speak of his 'metaphysic of light'. But this is too remote a concept. He began with something that was immediately present to him in everyday experience, in his scientific work, and in the Bible. The three parts of the Bible on which his theology was chiefly based – the Creation narrative in Genesis, the Psalms, and St John's Gospel and Epistles – are the source of all his theological thinking about light: 'Let there be light' (Genesis 1:3), 'the Lord is my light' (Ps 27:1), and a multitude of phrases from St John – 'I have come as light into this world', 'the true light', 'the true light which lighteth every man, that cometh into the world', and so on – established light as a central feature in his biblical theology. There is no need to look beyond this combination of common experience, science and biblical doctrine to understand Grosseteste's mature thought about light.[7]

Grosseteste's work on light, light as it affirms the contingency of creation to and from its Creator, disposing and ordering its entities in the integrity of their created verities, establishing the unity and diversity of all things that are in the Rationality of the uncreated Light of God, the Word come into his own domain, stands in that long line of truly κατα φυσιν thinking out of which Einstein could write of the verities of the universe, that they evoke that humble attitude of mind towards the grandeur of reason incarnate in existence, and which, in its profoundest depths, is inaccessible to man[8]; and the rapturous amazement at the harmony of natural law, which reveals an intelligence of such superiority that, compared with it, all systematic thinking and acting of human beings is an utterly insignificant reflection[9].

6

Light, Words and the Word of God

IN SUBSTANCE theological language is no different from any other form of written or spoken communication. It is not to be regarded as a field and dimension of human expression which is superior to normal usage; much less is it to be construed as of divine dimension. It is not the prelapsian language of Eden; it undoubtedly shares the idiom of all the confusions, constrictions, obstinacies and absurdities of the day by day existence and experience of Adamic flesh and nature.

Words by themselves are constrictions. They describe and define; by their very utterance they limit. That limitation becomes all the more obvious in the difficulty of translating from one language to another, for the definition of an object or an action by a word from one tongue is not necessarily consistent with the approximate equivalent from another. Indeed the use of words in communication by two individuals sharing a common speech can lead to a misunderstanding, for one person has his or her own understanding born of personal limitations or experiences necessarily imposed upon a particular word, and this individual nuance may not immediately be discernible to another.

The words used in theological language have not escaped the consequences of the fall of the tower of Babel. Indeed, when employed theologically, words can be dangerously close in intent to the end to which the very bricks and bitumen used in the construction of that edifice were directed.

Words are the audible and communicable expression of thoughts. There has to be a corresponding rationality between thought and the expression of it. But the thought itself, if it be rational, has to be formed by the compulsive reality of the object to which mental endeavour and assessment is directed. This we have looked at in terms of the unity and diversity of light both illuminating the object and enlightening the mind affixed in scrutinizing it, in a union whereby the object and the mental image granted by sight are joined as one instantaneously. But that does not complete and exhaust the role and action of light. The resultant thought has to be referred back again and again to the reality of the object, and tested for its valid rationality against the inherent integrity of the object as it unfolds itself under the revealing qualities of light in all the integrity of what it is in itself and in its light determined relation to its context.

To communicate the discernment of this reality in the interaction of the thinking subject with the objective realities, to interpret and to communicate their integrities and so for human beings to further react in the understanding of, respect for, and appreciation of relation to, them, words are required.

There is a correspondence in the relation of light and word and thought, at this created level where we live now, more, have our being and exercise our created rationality as thinking beings, to the consubstantiality between Father and Son in the bond of the Spirit whereby the Son, as the Word of the Father, is 'Light of Light'. Of course the human word is not as the divine Word, for, as the Image of God, he is what he images – for he is the perfect unity between Image and Substance, for he 'is of one substance with the Father', yet is 'the image of the Father'. But in our case, because of the refracted nature of the created dimension, word and object are separate, and may only be joined in the rational activity of the thinking subject as and by the rational activity of light-informed thought.

There is, then, a necessary relation of word to light, for words become the articulation of light-created thoughts about light-created and lightened realities. But this is not always recognized. The necessary context and order of objects as being within the intelligibility of a light-ordered creation, with all the marvellous and rational harmony of inter-locking fields of existence, which in their totality and in their diversity point to their contingency to and from uncreated Light as the Creator Word of God, is displaced by a merely observational, pragmatic and even utilitarian, approach, in which the essential bond between object and thinking subject is construed in terms of 'it' and 'me', a sort of Nestorian disjunction is isolated, self-contained units.

Words are then used to witness to particular reflections of light, that is objects or concerns in artificial isolation, rather than as reflections of that light, to light itself, and the fields of rationality as the context in which these objects or concerns can only be understood in their integrities and verities. Words become obdurate mirrors of what is perceived by the mind of the scrutinizing person to be merely three-dimensional existence – in the last resort mechanical and static vehicles of quantitivity, the jargon of a short sighted technological approach to all that is.

When this method of employing words as expressions of quantitative evaluation and description is applied to a consideration of creation in its entirety, we are faced with the three-dimensional absurdities. The totality of all creation can only be perceived in observational and mechanical terms, and in the projection of laws already formulated out of this attitude, as ultimates of reality. All the absurdities which this involves when this procedure is applied to God is heightened, for it involves the projection of three-dimensional existences on to God, who is ascribed as being, and interpreted accordingly, as but time and space writ large. It is here that the unthinking application of words such as 'infinity' and 'eternity' is seen at its platitudinous worst.

I have already touched on the unthinking use of the terms 'infinity' and 'eternity' in *The Dynamism of Space*. These, as they are habitually used, seem to me to be essentially comments on the limitations of our minds and an acknowledgement that language cannot cope with that which is beyond the constraints of our existence and experience, rather than appropriate attributes of God. By this usage, God is conceived as being beginningless and endless time and space. The only difference between such a deity and us is that we have a beginning and an end in the temporal/spatial realities which are our lot, while he has not. There is therefore only a quantitative difference between God and ourselves.

That scientific thought can regard even what we call 'time' and 'space' to be a dynamic and relational time/space continuum to be understood out of radically more than the

mechanical concepts of three-dimensional rigidities, is something which has not yet penetrated the general awareness and
expression of theological thought. In the exercise of theology,
a great deal of the Newtonian and Kantian attitudes (even if
a considerable number of the practitioners of theology have
not the ability to recognize them as such) which, in one form
or another, lie behind accepted thought patterns, have to be
excised if any credibility is to be given to theological understanding of reality.

Newton's system of thought equated God with an infinite,
unchanging framework of absolute, mathematical time and
space, to which relative, apparent time and space, charac-
terised by the motion and change of bodies, was to be
referred for understanding. This absolute, mathematical time
and space was the container in which, and the immutable
frame of reference by which, the relative time and space of
our experience and existence could be understood in a reduction of it to mathematically mechanistic calculation and
static formulae.

That the whole temporal/spatial universe was so contained
and controlled by this deified, unchangeable and impassible,
absolute time and space, meant that time and space became
rigorous categories identified ultimately with the inexorable
and unyielding mind and presence of God. This was why
Newton could not see the possibility of God incarnate, for
how could such a deity, containing all things, become something which he contained?

Coupled to this is the legacy of Kant who relocated the
concept of absolute time and space from God to the human
mind. Through this view, mechanistic thinking became even
more deeply entrenched in the ways and directions of
modern thought, for now the mind, with what was claimed
to be its inherent forms of intuitive capacities, and with its
unchanging structures of consciousness, which were identified with time and space, became the determiner of the
patterns of reality. The mind imposes laws on nature; it does
not perceive them out of nature. The reality of creation is the
order we lay upon it. Thus objectivity is reduced to subjective
consciousness.

When it comes to thinking about the incarnation in

Kantian mode, then we are faced with having to acknowledge that we can know nothing about it in or from itself,
except through what we impose upon the interpretation
already imposed upon it by the New Testament witnesses.

The combination of the legacies left by those two intellectual giants, so influential in and beyond their respective ages,
and the authors of much that is of value in many concerns,
has, however, produced a deeply-rooted residue of subjective, mechanized ways of thinking and of perceiving reality.
That this unfortunately colours common thinking, and has
penetrated into the area of theological thought, is all too
evident.

That scientific thinking has now overturned such an attitude, though it can be still entrenched there particularly in
the field of the technological sciences, has meant that an
imperative to reconsider what the reality of creation is, and
how to look at and consider it, is placed firmly before theology. Creation is the area where theological studies and scientific endeavour overlap.

That overlapping, and the mutual help that the one discipline can be to the other, can be seen even in the embryonic
work of Grosseteste's *De Luce*, and has been instanced by
those who are like-minded in both disciplines as to the mode
of perceiving the amazing harmonies and order of objective
realities grounded in their rationality beyond themselves,
throughout the ages, In more recent times and from both
disciplines, the work and contributions of M. Faraday, J.
Clerk Maxwell in the last century, N. Bohr, I. Prigogine, M.
Polanyi, T. F. Torrance, J. Polkinghorne, Paul Davies, to cite
but a sample of significant names, and now an increasing
number of people, have had, and do have, a wholesome and
beneficent achievement in regard to the advantages mutually
offered in the converse between science and theology.

These benefits only come, however, when the integrity of
both theology and science is maintained, and mutual respect
accorded. For the procedure of thought and resultant word,
while in both light-based in terms of what has been set out
above, are different. The one begins with the light of the
objective verities of creation in differentiation from God, as
they unfold themselves in all their rationality of what they

are in themselves, and yet, in their contingent rationality point to an ultimate intelligible ground, the other with what it confesses to be that ultimate intelligible Ground, the light of the Word as uncreated Light made flesh in the midst of the structures of his own creation. From their respective starting points both disciplines, hopefully, travel, meet and embrace and converse. The concourse where this takes place is the structure of the created entities in all their harmony and order, which theology confesses and professes to be the handiwork of God embraced in his Incarnate Word, and which both view as characterized by the rationality of light.

While κατα φυσιν thinking is the hallmark of both disciplines, the objects illuminating their respective thoughts and the words, correspondingly employed in propriety to the nature of these objects as expressions of these thoughts, are different. Pure physics, astrophysics, etc., express these thoughts mathematically in the first instance. As T. F. Torrance has pointed out[1], in these scientific disciplines, the physical properties of light, because of light's nature and behaviour, moving as it does and conveying information, require mathematical expression if they are to be analysed and understood. Thus, light coming from all parts of the universe and bearing data from its source, before this information can be articulated, has first to come through the medium of mathematical formulae. Numbers are then transformed into words which express the nature of the objective realities of which light, formulated into mathematical indications, is the agent witnessing to these realities and serving us by transmitting knowledge of them. This procedure is not an exercise in abstraction; meaningless outside itself; it is the particular way in which the bond between the thinking subject and the objective verities articulating themselves by light, is forged, and the thoughts so articulated in words out of numbers by the subject made the servants of the objective verities.

It has to be noted that there is an interdependence between number and word. Number is that which, in scientific endeavour, anchors word and gives it content and direction – it is the discipline behind word; but word is that which intelligibly expresses number and opens it out to greater possibilities than it possesses in itself. A mathematical formula is a formal, impersonal and incomplete statement, essentially detached from the objective reality it describes as but a description of it. Translated into word, it becomes a rational, verbal statement anchored to, and ontologically concerned with, the existence of the objective reality, open to, and serving the understanding of a more complete and wider rationality. Apart from this, it can then interact with other disciplines to its own enrichment and more comprehensive understanding.

Theology, on the other hand, does not operate with numbers. But its employment of words is (or ought to be) no less rigorous. It, I would suggest, has to handle its sources, in this case the biblical witnesses to God's Self-revelation, in their preparatory form in the Old Testament, and in their recollective form in the New Testament, in a particular way. Clearly, these sources bear all the hallmarks of historical and cultural contexts, and the nature of these has to be taken into account. But they are not mere records and instances of such. They are directed beyond their context of cultural norms and historical exigencies, and, in this paradeigmatic activity, are indeed assayers of what moulds and forms and brings about their respective, and therefore all, cultures and movements of human circumstance.

Athanasius was quite clear as to what the scriptures were pointing, and this he described as their σκοπος – *skopos, scope.* This means much more than our common usage of the word 'scope'. It indicates the inner content, the centre, the horizon and the goal. This *skopos* is the Word of God made flesh[2].

But Athanasius uses the word 'scope' in another application related to this. The σκοπος of the Word made flesh is also the perspective within which scriptural statements are significant and comprehensible, and theological statements, from their biblical matrix, are likewise intelligible and of propriety. This means that the 'scope' determines their place and relation to each other.

Perhaps the best way to think about this double meaning of σκοπος is to think of a wheel, with its spokes going to the hub from the rim – an illustration of theological procedure

and one which, I am well aware, has limitations and contradictions inherent in it, but I nevertheless offer it. In this illustration, we may think of the hub as God as he is in himself,
in se, and the rim as God as he is *ad extra*, the incarnation,
God, of course, being towards us in Jesus Christ what he is in
himself. The point is that the spokes may be regarded as
statements which are directed towards the hub, but their
direction, shape and size, their paradeigmatic value, are
determined by the rim holding them to the hub. But the rim
also determines their place and relation to each other, so that
they all are complementary, and form a perfect circle in their
harmony and singleness of purpose in their multiplicity.

Not only the rationality of theological statements as they
take their origin from the nature of their 'scope' and are
formed in all propriety by its Rationality, but the rationality
of theological articulations in their relation to each other, as
complementary statements supporting each other by their
individual and collective order and so mutually witnessing to
the overall order of the whole endeavour in the knowledge of
God, are thus formed. Should one spoke be too long, or too
short, it must be made to fit in accordance both with the axle
and the rim and in trim with its fellows.

But it will be noted that in this illustration, the spokes both
come and go from hub to rim and rim to hub. The human
endeavour in all this is that if we treat the spokes as illumination from God, it is by way of our participation in Christ
that we can only properly make them our own and only
fittingly direct them back to God as statements about him.

This presupposes two things: first that knowledge is in the
context of an actual living relation with God as he is in
himself and as he is in the Word made flesh; second that faith
that this is illumination from God is necessary as a precondition to understanding. These two factors are interlinked and
mutually necessary.

The Self-revelation and Self-giving of God determines the
witness to himself, its nature and mode of expression. It is
the mould in which concepts and words, in all their impropriety and inadequacy to signify the God who is beyond
comparison, are bent out of their normal usage to serve in an
appropriate manner as possible the God who is indescrib-

able. It is that which determines the way in which human language is qualified and directed in its inadequacy to speak of the Being of God as he is in himself, as the Triune God. For the incarnation is the Self-revelation and Self-giving of that God which has taken the totality of our being to himself, making our creaturely existence one of 'godliness' corresponding to his 'Godness' and creating in us the capacity to bear witness in our concepts and words in propriety with his Self-witness. That which primarily bears upon our concepts and words, marshalling, reforming and redirecting them, in the governance of the Word made flesh, is them Holy and Undivided Trinity.

This is why Irenaeus, at the very beginning of his *Demonstration of the Apostolic Preaching*, is so insistent that the knowledge of God is a matter of lively 'godliness', that is in a living relation with God in which human life and endeavour is in correspondence with the Godness of God, as God exists in himself. It is no good, says Irenaeus, if we have truth of God in the soul, that is the mind, and that truth is contradicted by the rest of our existence. Nor is it any good if our outward piety by which we deport ourselves and seek to please God is contradicted by the fact that we have no knowledge of God in the mind. As he says of this totality of knowledge and being in its relation to God:

> The glory of God is a living man, and the life of man consists in beholding God.[3]

Knowledge of God is necessarily participation in the life of God and the knowledge which he has of himself, which participation comes by the incarnation of the Word embracing to himself the totality of human existence, so that knowledge of God is not an abstraction, a disinterested objectivity, but the very presence and life of God brought to bear on our existence and giving it light reflected back to him.

The statements of theological language are then to be understood as of double contingence – they are utterly dependent upon God for their illumination, yet are made ours in their created dimension and creaturely correspondence to the nature of their source and goal.

It is this primary direction of language humanward by

God, giving it distinctive usage and content, rather than only a direction of language directed and determined by humanity Godward, which Irenaeus sees as a necessity. In this particular instance Irenaeus emphasizes the difference between 'word' as a created human expression with all its temporal limitations, and 'the uncreated Word' as God's being and act.[4]

> Just as he does not err who declares that God is all vision, and all hearing (for in what manner He hears, in that also He sees), so also he who affirms that He is all intelligence, and all word, and that, in what respect He is intelligence, in that also He is word, and that this Nous is His Logos, will still indeed have an inadequate conception of the Father of all, but will entertain far more becoming [thoughts regarding Him] than do those who transfer the generation of the word to which men give utterance to the Word of God, assigning a beginning and course of production [to Him], even as they do to their own words. And in what respect will the Word of God – yea, rather God Himself, since He is the Word – differ from the word of men, if He follows the same order and process of generation?

A two-fold requirement of care with words as used theologically is set out by Irenaeus. First, the limitations of words as anchored in, and limited by, the temporal/spatial dimension, cannot be transferred as they are commonly formulated and used within that dimension, to the Being of God. Second, the proper formulation and usage of them consists in a recognition of their created content as created expressions and a bending and direction of that usage which does not convey that created content into God.

Athanasius takes this further, and underlines both this and the necessity of a careful choice of words if they are to be appropriate images pointing truly to God. This choice is determined by the nature of God as he is revealed in the incarnation, and through the flesh of the Word in its union with the Word, words are taken up as true paradeigmatic signs to the Being of God as he is in himself. Even then, they are not conclusions about God, only pointers to him.

Both Athanasius, John Chrysostom and Cyril of Alexandria are also clear that the theological mind is the biblical mind. The terminology biblically applied to the

Word made flesh, and through, in and by him moulded into symbols which in the propriety to that Self-revelation are applicable to God as he is in himself, is to be followed in theological endeavour.

It was this awareness and perception which caused such great hesitation about the inclusion of the ομοουσιον ('of one substance') in the Creed formulated at the Council of Nicaea in AD325, in applying it to the relation of the Son to the Father and the Father to the Son. It was not strictly speaking biblical, in that it does not appear explicitly in scripture. It was accepted on the grounds that it was the distillation of the scriptural emphasis in such text as *I and the Father are one*. Indeed, the whole Creed was regarded as a faithful distillation and concentration of scriptural meaning and usage. But the agonizing and the argument which gathered round the use of the ομοουσιον demonstrates the care and concern regarding the propriety of words and statements in accord with the biblical mode of witnessing κατα φυσιν, to the nature and substance of the incarnation.

Athanasius's constant warning against the Arian carelessness (see especially *Contra Arianos in passim*), in using words and concepts in their common application and understanding, that is, in their created limitations and connotations, indiscriminately and directly of God instead of a careful choice of appropriate words as paradeigmatically applied to God, is paralleled in the summary injunction of Ambrose[6]:

> Cease then to apply to the Godhead that which is proper only to created existences.

It should be remarked that Athanasius's views of such Arian aberration (as Irenaeus's concerning Gnostic claims) where that this both disparaged the existence of humanity and the existence of God, doing harm to the integrities of both in their respective identities and natures.

As to the care in choice of appropriate verbal symbols, Grosseteste was later to wax eloquent on the care needed in establishing propriety, and the need for awareness of the inherent impropriety and limitations in all such. For they are expressions of human being, part of the totality which that being is in all its frailty and mortality, trying to speak of that which is the Source of all being, and is Being itself without beginning and end and who is the Beginning and the End.

Without degenerating his argument into a theological *via negativa*, whereby God is perceived to be not what everything else is (an argument which Gregory Nazianzen refuted by sharply pointing out, in company with Athanasius and Basil, that if we cannot say anything positive as to what God is, then we cannot say with any accuracy what he is not[6]) – Grosseteste says that the negation of all things is true of God. But this is in the context of his thesis that all affirmative symbols ascribed to God are false when *literally*, that is, still in their accepted, common understanding, affirmed of God.

Grosseteste emphasizes that any understanding of the material, earthly content of words and statements and symbols has to be excised from the mind, if they are to be directed to God. Moreover, there is a great danger is using the more immaterial images of, for example, light or the heavens. For these approximate more by even their created nature, purer and more 'spiritual' than gross symbols and the words expressing these, to the being of God who is over and above and beyond all created things in his existence *in se*. This concern as to care in the choice and application of verbal images and of symbols to God is evident throughout his *Commentary on the Celestial Hierarchies* and especially so in the fifteenth chapter of that work. In all this he is well aware that the context of the suitability of statements applied to God is the relation of created existence as such to the uncreated Existence which God is, and the creaturely correspondence of the former to the latter.

So too in the matter of knowledge's presupposition of faith, it is perhaps in Anselm's *Proslogion* that we find the dilemma of the human being, in its frail and mortal state with its lapsed and limited mind, engaged in the pursuit of the knowledge of God in its relation to faith, best expressed. This is done with recource to the metaphor of light.

7

Light, Words, Understanding and the Knowledge of God

ANSELM declares (*Proslogion*: Preface) that after the many connected arguments on the meaning of faith which he had marshalled in his previous work, the *Monologion*, he sought one single argumentfor the existence of God, an argument *requiring no proof other than itself*. This is an important qualifying phrase, for it demonstrates how he perceived the nature of the definitive phrase, the single argument which he is about to conclude.

After the Preface, there follows the account of his odyssey[1] in which his search for this is revealed in all the poignancy of his endeavour:

> Surely you dwell in inaccessible light; where is it? and how can I have admittance to light which is inaccessible?
> Who will lead me and take me into it that I may thus see you there?

This is in the context of a musing as to his limitations and frailties, what good he has coming only from God, which assail and make impossible the fulfilment of that for which he was created and re-created:

> I was created to see you, and I have not yet accomplished that for which I was made. How miserable is the lot of man when he has lost the very thing for which he was created.[2]

This universal estate of humanity is not only the result of the common Adamic human folly (c.f., eg 63-64; 96-98), but of God's judgement on that recapitulative turning from him by Adam.

> Why did he revoke our light and encompass us with darkness? Why did he take away our life and give us the wound of death?[3]
> ... from the vision of God into our self-blindness?[4]

What Anselm laments here is that alienation of the creature from the Creator, and the inability of the mind, in that fallen estate, to perceive and know God in the uncreated Light which he is in himself. It is only God who, by looking upon us, can enlighten and reveal himself, so that prayer must be for that turning of God's face towards us that we may see his light in whatever state we are, and that God himself will teach us to seek him and in that seeking show himself.[5] This echoes the whole Old Testament emphasis of the face of God being turned towards humanity for humanity's enlightenment and that the way in which humanity should walk be made plain.

For Anselm that seeking is not a desire to rise to the heights of God, for the darkened understanding of the creature will not allow this. It is a seeking to *understand* what is already, however, tenuously, believed and loved:

> I do not understand so that I may believe, but I believe so that I may understand; and moreover, I believe that unless I do believe I shall not understand.[6]

This is *Fides Quaerens Intellectum, Faith Seeking Understanding*, Anselm's entitling of this book.[7] It is here that his *single argument ... requiring no proof other than itself*, is introduced. This statement came to him (as noted by his own admission and in the record of Eadmer in chapter XIX of the latter's *Vita S. Anselmi*), as an illumination while engaged in the office of Matins. Although he had tried to put the idea of such an argument out of his mind, it pressed upon him, urgently importuning and compelling him, and wearing out his resistance to it.[8] In other words, it came to Anselm despite himself, and he views it as that which is given him from God rather than a construct of his own devising. It came by way of enlightenment.

It consists in the belief that God is *that, more than which nothing greater can be thought*.[9] In it is contained the faith

> that you exist as we believe, and that you are what we believe you to be.[10]

But what of the fool who, according to the Psalmist, says in his heart *There is no God*? Anselm points out that when a like foolish person hears him say that God is *that, more than which nothing greater can be thought,* by hearing it, it enters his understanding, but (and here is the crisis of this particular argument) it cannot exist *only* in the understanding, for something greater than that which exists *only* in the understanding can be thought, namely, that which exists in reality and not only in the understanding.

This is later clarified further:

> Then you are, Lord, not merely that than which nothing greater can be thought; you are even that which is greater than it is possible to think about. Since then it is possible to think that this could exist, then, should you be not this, a greater than you could be thought, and this could not be so.[11]

Without doubt, the statement that what Anselm was seeking was an argument *requiring no proof other than itself* is applicable to this argument which he finally advocates, the belief that God is *that, more than which nothing greater can be thought.* For it bears within itself its own proof of itself, in that in whatever way it may be sought to be contradicted, it contradicts that contradiction, for any contradiction of it can always be shown by the very statement contradicted to be lesser than it and inadequate to answer it.

This is not meant to be a detailed interpretation of Anselm; rather the employment of some questions suggested in this particular work here as suggestive pointers to wider issues in the question of the relation of faith to understanding and both to knowledge. For several issues, it seems to me, underlie his thought.

These are: that in the way he sets out his description of his search for this foolproof argument, it may be thought that he is taking it for granted that there is a God of a certain qualitative existence as is appropriate for an assumed Creator; and also, it should be noted, that he puts the development of his argument into the context of light.

With regard to the first, I would suggest that Anselm is treating belief here not as some blind, abstract and indescribable hope, but as the necessary intuitive ground on which understanding becomes possible. Perhaps we may illustrate this in this way; as we grow from infancy to childhood, the objective realities of the context in which we so develop impinge upon us, pressing in, so that we not only intuitively

perceive their significance, but also intuitively obey the physical laws which govern that context and our existence within
it. All this we do intuitively as we relate to these verities and
laws, without either intelligible acknowledgement or rational
formulation of them. A child learning to walk commits itself
unknowingly to more laws of physics than could ever be
articulated.

In the same way we intuitively are in touch with the verities of realities greater than our conceptualized understanding of them, and here the second issue lying behind Anselm's
thought comes to the fore. For it is significant that he puts
the working out of his argument into the context of light –
the enlightenment of the mind, our need for light both
mental and physical, the unapproachable light of God, and
that he construes existence, either creaturely or divine, in
terms of light.

Light, again I would suggest, is that which we intuitively
perceive as the ground of understanding, and the need of
humanity (acknowledged or not) for light and enlightenment
points both to the necessity of seeing understanding and
knowledge anchored in the rational light-ordered existence,
and cries out for the ultimate Rationality in which this has its
source, its meaning and its purpose.

This is faith, which is the necessary precondition of understanding, and the field in which rationality operates to
achieve the understanding of what is so believed. As understanding is thus achieved, there is a purifying process
whereby faith is winnowed, false belief removed and true
belief made even more suitable for yielding yet more understanding.

This faith is an awareness of the relation of being to being.
Anselm knows in faith the relation of humanity to God, and
it is this he seeks to understand. But he is always aware of the
limitations of the whole estate of humanity which includes
the mind, and the impossibility of humanity achieving a true
and complete understanding and knowledge of God, but
always going on in faith to deeper faith. For he is also aware
that God, if he is God, can only truly know God, and that
only God can impart this knowledge which he has of himself
by giving us to share in it.

It is the goodness of God which accomplishes this, and that goodness, according to Anselm, is the way in which God exists as Father and Son bound in the bond of divine Love, the Holy Spirit, proceeding from the Father through the Son.[12] The Word which God utters is nothing less than himself. It is this which faith desires, and in the granting of it to the faith which it has evoked so that it is intuitive, there is given the way to understanding and understanding itself. This is within an awareness of the relation of created existences to the Creator as a relation of contingency. God is all goodness and blessedness in himself:

> you yourself are ... entirely sufficient to yourself, in need of nothing, yet he whom all things need for their being and well-being.[13]

Anselm is clear that understanding is never merely conceptual. This is why his one single argument that God is that than which nothing greater can be thought, cannot exist merely as an idea in the mind; by its very nature it confounds such attempts to so contain and constrict it, and refutes any idea that the understanding can ever comprehend the existence of God within its creaturely capacities. It is not only an ontological statement, for it is a statement about statements concerning God and the human mind, and, as such, is a statement which concerns the relational rationalities (rather than only ontologically, the rational relations) of the existence of God and humanity.

Understanding and knowledge takes place primarily because of the faithfulness of God, as constant Light, creating and granting that Light's creaturely correspondence of its constancy, which is faith. Through faith, the perception of our living context is directed to where uncreated Light, as the Word, is made flesh and gathers our existence into the embrace of his uncreated Existence. The Christocentricity of Anselm is stated and affirmed strongly in his *Cur Deus Homo?*, as it is in the precis of part of that work, his *Meditation on Human Redemption*. It is in Christ, as the faithfulness of God, that faith is created, though we understand that not at all. Thus pointed to him, in the consideration of human need and divine faithfulness, it is

created anew in him, the light of understanding in the
enlightenment of the mind given to that faith by him, and
words and statements become possible as enlightened and
enlightening, in turn the created correspondences of the
uncreated Rationality and Light of him as the Word, one
with the Father and the Spirit.

The example of Anselm's argument may be used as a
demonstration that, just as science cannot operate with
number only, neither can theology be reduced to concept.
Both theology and science would then be mere abstractions.
Number, mathematical formulae as information about some
object or objects, has to be interpreted by word as a
paradeigmatic statement pointing to the existence and nature
of the objective of the objective realities articulating themselves by light in their inherent and relational rationality, and
thus, by word, becomes more than mere abstraction.
Number, interpreted by word, becomes the faithful servant
of those realities as they are in themselves in the fullness of
their intelligible existences, and, being so interpreted by
word, becomes the bond between objective, light-articulated
intelligibility and thinking subject enlightened by that light –
and, it may be added, but by no means as a mere addition,
enlightened by the intuitive reasoning of the mind,
profoundly related to light as the rational existence of
humanity. Science, too, has its faith, the context by which it
comes to disciplined understanding.

Theology cannot, or should not if it is theology, be the
merely conceptual. But because it does not operate with
number, which gives direction to word, it has to be even
more careful in its handling of words. It is all too easy for
word and thought to degenerate into, and rest content with
being merely conceptual. Faith demands that, if word and
thought are to lead to understanding, they must be seen as
the servants of the relational rationalities of the Existence of
the living God who has uttered his Word amid the structures
and existences of this world, and of this created existence of
ours by which we live and move and have our being, and
think and speak out of faith that we might understand.
Understanding comes through faith which is directed by and
in light to its source, the incarnation of uncreated Light as

the Word, the Rationality of God, on whom all light and understanding depend. In his Light we see light and understand that this light is the well of life, the life of all creation in its relation to its Creator.

But all this rests on the assumption that light is communicated from and to existences in a particular way. How is this done and in what way? We have seen already how Robert Grosseteste grasped and set out the dependence of our way of attaining knowledge on the quality and action of light. This he did in terms of the relation between the mind (via the sight), the objective observed, and the unity of the mental image of that object perceived and that object itself. With the emphasis of Anselm on light and being discussed above in mind, I would wish to take this further to indicate a perhaps wider and deeper factor with regard to light and understanding and knowledge.

I have claimed already that our thinking is created by light and participates in light itself. In other words, we have to do with a double contingency here also. We are dependent utterly upon light for our knowing; yet, within that dependency, the light-created knowing is *our* knowing – the way we think as different persons and the contribution we may make to knowledge by that individuality and particularity of thought.

But this knowledge is more than a matter of just seeing things and their context, physically. Light is bestowed upon us in the vast range of its quality and activity, for it is more than that which is to do with the sight of the eyes alone, having in its quality and nature so many wave-lengths and frequencies. It is bestowed on those who are blind in ways other than by the sight, so that blind individuals, sharing with everyone in the particularity of their personal thinking, have different and varied ways of 'looking' at things – ways which so often are revealing of a profundity of insight unappreciated by the sighted. A theology of light written by a blind theologian could well bring to light dimensions not otherwise perceived, just, indeed, as a theology of word could by one profoundly deaf.

I would put it forward that this bestowing and activity of light so initiates and sustains our way of knowing, that this mode of our knowledge is related to light in such a degree that it takes its pattern from the property and action of light. And more than this, for light gathers up the rational processes of human existence which it has initiated and called forth, establishing and forming them as their ground and their source, yet adapting itself to particular individuality, so that that individual becomes a personal servant of truth mediated by light.

But created light, in all its forms and range, is itself grounded on the uncreated Light of God who brings it into being and bestows its quality, nature and role, and to whom it points as the Author, Establisher and Perfecter of all. Light is also, in its relation to uncreated Light, the characteristic of created being, the ground whereby all creation is constituted as a rational existence. And, by its processes, engendering our understanding and creating our knowing of the created verities in their contingent relation to the Creator, evoking the rightness of our responses to them and to the Creator.

Here we have to do with different levels of truth and rationality – of the Creator, of creation and of our knowing. These levels are set out in Anselm's *De Veritate*, and I use his distinction of Highest, Ultimate or Supreme Truth, truth of created existences and truth of our statements, as a spur to further thought.

T. F. Torrance has analyzed these Anselmic distinctions in his *Reality and Evangelical Theology*,[14] beginning with the observation that Anselm operated with a definition of truth as 'rightness', and that his 'rightness' of truth is expressed through a hierarchical dependence – not a static but an active hierarchy, it must be added – in which the *truth of signification* (the truth of our statements) depends on the *truth of things*, which in turn depends on the *Supreme Truth of God*, which, in its Self-sufficiency, depends on nothing.

1. **The truth of signification**. This concerns our statements about objects. These statements have an indebtedness to the object to which they are directed, for the object demands our true acknowledgement of it. We must not disparage or demean it by stating that it is what it is not. In being faithful towards its objective verity, we give it its right place and due, and so there will be a rapport of exactitude between the

object and our statements concerning it. This, of course, is κατα φυσιν thinking – thinking out of a centre which is the nature of that object, and allowing what it is in itself to displace all our presuppositions and preconceptions. It follows that the truth of any statement we may make on this basis lies primarily not in the statement itself, but in that statement's faithfulness to the object as it really is in itself and as it has disclosed itself, on its own terms, to be. The rightness of our statement will be its exactitude towards the objective verity.

The authority of our statement, then, is the authority of the integrity of the object reflected by that statement. There is a process of 'justification', in the proper sense of 'putting right' or 'being right with', here, whereby the rightness of the statement is justified by the verity of the object. That the rightness, truth and authority of our statement are derived from the integrity of the object, and therefore secondary to the rightness, truth and authority of that object, is, if we think about it, abundantly evident from the fact that the object was what it is, is what it is, and will be what it is, before we began to think and speak about it, while we are thinking and speaking about it, and long after we have ceased to think and speak about it. The object, in the majesty, dignity and authority of its integrity, does not require our statements for it to be what it is; whereas we require its integrity for the rightness and truth of our statements.

There is, however, according to Anselm, another respect in which a statement can be said to be 'right'. A statement cannot be applied to a rational end, that is the right signification of an object, unless it itself is rational – that is, makes grammatical sense being a coherent sequence of intelligible words. It must possess an intelligibility of its own. But it seems to me that even here the objective verity of that to which the statement is directed will dictate and control the very fabric of that statement. It will demand a propriety of words – nouns, adjectives, verbs, adverbs, which are suitable to its nature. There is a pattern of double contingency here also, that the rationality of a sentence or statement is evident from within itself, but is as nothing unless it is in relation to the objective rationality. The truth of signification, therefore, depends upon the truth of things, for statements are evoked by, faithfully constructed in accordance with, and meaningfully applied to, those things.

2. **The truth of things.** This is construed by Anselm as objects being what they are and should be, in strict accord with their natures. When they are so, they exist 'rightly'. The truth of a thing is defined as the integrity of it as it exists rightly, and not as something other than its nature requires it to be. But this integrity is held by things from God; it is not an integrity that can be seen as self-sufficient or autonomous, but is to be understood as theirs in their contingent relation to God their Creative Ground and Source. Their 'rightness', the integrity which they have being what they are, is paradeigmatic. For they are what they truly are only in relation to the Supreme Truth, the Ground and Cause of their truth, to whom they are therefore indebted for what they are.

But this pointing beyond themselves to the Supreme Truth does not mean that the created entities are mere signs, empty of any content or purpose. It does mean that the truth of what they really and actually are in their propriety and place in the created order and as integrally part of it, has this paradeigmatic quality and role by necessity. They would not be created entities with particular purposes and places in the created dimension, otherwise. For they exist, and can only exist, in a double contingency to and from God, and their truth of what they are in themselves signifies that they are grounded beyond themselves in the Supreme Truth of their Creator.

So far, in both these categories, the truth of signification and the truth of things, we have an hierarchical indebtedness, an obligation and dependency: that is, created existences owe the rightness of what they really and actually are to the Supreme Truth to which they point as the Ground of that existence and identity; and statements owe their rightness to the objective verities of created existences as they are in relation to that Supreme Truth and as they point to it. In both cases, it is on that Supreme Truth as Author and Goal, that their respective 'rightnesses' fundamentally and ultimately depend. It is the coping-stone which holds them in 'rightness' and on and in which, rising up as pointers to it, they rest.

3. **The Supreme Truth of God.** This is not on the same level as, and competing on equal terms with, other truths. For this Truth is the 'Rightness' of God's Being which is in distinction to all other beings, yet to which they are related as their Source, Sustainer and Perfecter of their existence, rightness and truth. This Truth is alone Self-existent, Self-sufficient, and Autonomous. This Truth of God is indebted to nothing other than himself, and is caused by nothing other than his own Existence. Indeed, it is his Existence.

All other truths are indebted to it, for they are not self-creating, self-propagating and self-maintaining. Their existence and the rightness of it are caused and effected by this Supreme Truth as a created existence and rightness corresponding in its finite and creaturely state to his uncreated Existence and Rightness.

But what of theological statements which are statements about this Supreme Truth? How can they speak of uncreated Light, since none can approach this? Moreover, since God is *that, more than which nothing greater can be thought ... even that which is greater than it is possible to think about,* are we not faced with a qualitative barrier against which all our statements, even for all their rightness pointing to the Supreme Truth of God, must dash themselves in wasted silence? How can we express the Rationality of God, which, as Anselm himself admits, is so deep and broad that it cannot at all be fathomed by human mental endeavour? Here we may take into account what Anselm emphasizes throughout his main works, that there is a relation of a radical kind between forms of words (*locutio*) and thought and rationality (*ratio*) and the existence of objective verities. These objective truths determine our mode of thinking and speaking about them. I have written already about existences calling to each other, and I am sure that this is what Anselm had in mind when he speaks of this relation between word, thought and rationality and existences. That is to say that word is embedded in being. Existences are not dumb; they have their natural inner voice and speech. This speech is of a kind not immediately recognizable, for clearly it is not of the form and construction of the words and speech we daily use.

I put forward that there is a quality of articulation, of being able to communicate as it were (though this is not to be conceived of in any anthropomorphic way), inherent to existences by their very nature – qualitatively different between the divine Existence and created existences, and that this articulation is determined by light.

Perhaps the usage of the Hebrew language may best provide an entrance into what I mean. The word for 'word', *dābhār*, is not an abstraction. To utter a word is the active expression of a reality. The verbal form denoting the causative does not distinguish between *making* something and *saying* what that thing is. The word is the expression of the totality and essence of what it indicates. If I pronounce my name I express myself in my totality. This indication of the totality means that words are used to convey the relation between the abstract and the concrete in a different way than that by which we employ words. Thus *mlk*, the root that indicates anything to do with kingly quality, is variously organized to express 'king', 'kingship', 'kingdom' and the quality of acting as a king, and *tōbh*, is simultaneously 'goodness', that is the quality of being good, and a 'good person' – goodness in all its expressions. In all Semitic languages there is little differentiation between the various classes of words, each word being modified as the expression of a particular manifestation of the general. But for our purposes it is the relation of word to the entity it seeks to express, the unifying relation between thing signified and its signification, underlying this, which is important. Here, of course, we have been dealing with the human usage of words *about* things and the perception of these words in relation to the very essence of the realities they indicate.

I use this as an entrance into what I see as a further stage of this sort of relation between word and object and the understanding of that object κατα φυσιν. And that is that there is lodged within the very nature of the object, whatever it is, a rationality which is not mute but has the property of expressing itself. Here I am using 'word' to indicate 'fundamental rationality'.

God is not Wordless. His Word is his very Being and the expression of it. The Word is consubstantial, co-eternal with the Father and the Spirit and therefore exists in a totally different way, as Person, from the 'word' residing in created objects which can only indicate, in expressing their existence, that they are finite. He is *the* express Image of God; all other words, of whatever quality or usage are significations of being, closely related to that being, but not that being itself. As the rationality of that being or object, they are dependent upon the Word or Rationality of God, imaging in their created rationality, and pointing to, the divine Rationality which has bestowed and formed that created rationality.

Rationality calls out to rationality. Being, through this fundamental speech embedded in its very existence as the expression of what it truly and rightly is, 'speaks' to being. Our task is to translate that basic, primary 'speech' of existences, into our intelligible speech, formed rightly in accordance with the nature of that fundamental 'speech' of each object as it is in itself and in its relation to others in the totality of creation.

We cannot do this by imposing our own terms on the created verities; they call out of what they are and we must 'listen' to the expression of their rationality. But rationality is light-ordered and light-sustained. It is a communication of light in its illuminating and enlightening activity. Our understanding, therefore, is caused and effected, follows and is expanded by this activity of light, our own rationality answering the 'speech' of the rationality of the objects we study. Just as there are levels of truth – the Supreme Truth of God, the truth of things and the truth of statement – so there are levels of rationality differentiated by the nature and activity of light.

When we seek to listen to the Supreme Truth of God, there is, from our side, an impossible qualitative barrier which brings us to a silence. That happens when we seek the Supreme Truth of God as detached from how that Truth has expressed itself. For it has itself opened that barrier in the incarnation of the Word. The Supreme Truth of God confronts us and compels us to listen to it, the uncreated

Light of God as the Word of God, on its own terms. There the Rationality of God is translated for us in the Person, words and acts of Jesus Christ into the dimension of our rationality without ceasing to be what it is.

It is still the Rationality of God, beyond human endeavour to encompass within the limitations of our rationality, just as created light cannot outshine uncreated Light. But it opens out our rationality to itself so that we can understand it in the acknowledgement of the integrity of its Majesty, Authority and Lordship over all creation, our rationality included. This is the level of Supreme Truth, divine Rationality, uncreated Light, taking the level of created things to itself and bringing their truth, rationality and created light into relation with himself as their ground and source and fulfilment. In that light we can see the rationality embedded within creation and 'speaking' out to us in its own terms in relation to its Creator. The 'rightness' of our translating that rationality into intelligible statement, the third level of truth, then becomes possible.

Theological rationality, as part of that third level, listens to the biblical witness to the Word made flesh, to uncreated Light speaking in human voice as the provision made for us to hear. And we listen to these human words of the biblical witnesses, the rationality of their articulation being on the basis of that Speech in God and of God that has been heard, believed, wrestled with and turned into rightness of human statement under obedience to its Nature and faithfully pointing to it. The authority and rightness of scripture does not lie in itself, but in that to which it witnesses. This is its rationality, that amid all the very human circumstances to which it bears witness and in which it was written, and in all the very human limitations of how it was written, these, in the recording of their obedience or disobedience, their wisdom or their folly, their goodness or their sin, point in all this to the Rightness of God in his Being and acts toward and for creation. That is where the rationality of scripture is anchored, and, if attention is drawn from this essentially paradeigmatic rationality, and a rationality which is autonomous in scripture itself is sought, as both literalism and so many biblical 'critics' in their different ways so seek, then this is to irrationalize the bible and demean the nature from which it speaks.

In scripture, the consideration of all three levels of truth and rationality which is the 'speech' of light, gather together – the Supreme Truth, the uncreated Light of God as his Word, the light of scripture as words witnessing to the uncreated Light which is the Word, and the light of our statements which, hopefully in their rightness, interpret scripture in accordance with its paradeigmatic nature. Theology thereby rightfully advances in an understanding of God to the benefit of all who deal with the understanding of the nature of this creation in which we live, move and have our being in relation to the Father of our Lord Jesus Christ who in that Jesus has declared and shown himself, Word and Light, to be the faithful and loving Creator, who is his own interpreter and who has made plain his Truth and his very way for us in the Light of that Truth.

8

The 'Obscurism' of Light and the Nature of God

WHEN we speak of the incarnation of the Word, we refer to God's Self-revelation, God confronting us face to face. Here, and only here, does the possibility of understanding God emerge. But to understand God does not mean that we explain God totally, satisfactorily and in conclusion. It means to know God as he is and as he remains as he is – that than which no greater can be thought, even that which is greater than it is possible to think about. We can only know God on his own terms, and he comes to us as Lord over all our thoughts.

The revelation of God as the Word made flesh therefore confronts us with both an entrance into the knowledge of God and the barrier to an explanation of the mystery of God. He gives himself to us, but does not thereby give himself up to be bound by the constrictions of our understanding. This would presuppose that our thoughts are greater than God.

The uncreated Light of God both reveals and conceals. There is a parallel in the nature of created light to this, for it corresponds in its finite nature to that uncreated Light which called it into being, and is therefore helped to us in that correspondence as a pointer to the nature of the uncreated Light which God is. We have to do here with both clarity and obscurity.

I have already made excuse regarding the word 'obscurism', for it seems to me that as a term it best indicates an essential factor about the nature of physical or created light, namely that light itself is invisible. We may see the reflections of light as it illuminates objects, but it itself cannot be seen. Only as there is another element present in the path of a beam of light, particles of some substance, can

109

we perceive it as a ray, but, again, of itself, the beam is invisible. Light itself is utterly obscure.

But invisibility is not the only property of light which give it obscurity. Light has an obscuring effect, in that we cannot look directly at any created medium of intense, powerful light – the most brilliant natural medium in our case being the sun. To do so would be to damage and darken, bedazzle or even blind the sight. Yet sight itself is adapted to receive light. Light has a quality of excluding us from beholding it in its most brilliant expression. And this is only created light.

It is only as the sight is protected by something which intervenes between the eye and the source of light, can we look upon that source, and even then not in its full intensity. Equally, mediation of a different nature is required to translate invisible light into intelligible information. The 'obscurism' of light, then, refers to it being in its natural invisibility and intensity utterly elusive to us, both evading and forbidding our direct comprehension of it.

The theological employment of light as a paradeigmatic verbal illustration to point to the truth of God's uncreated Light utilizes the same elements of dark invisibility, overpowering intensity and the necessity of a protecting, interpreting mediator between God and humanity.

In biblical terms, the giving of the law through Moses is perceived to be such an intervening protection – a necessary medium between the uncreated Light of God in all his righteousness and humanity in all its frailty. The direct presence of that uncreated Light could not be borne by that created dimension of human existence and capability. Instead, the righteousness of God, with its impossible demand *Be ye holy as I am holy* is mediated through the precepts of the law, protectively directing humanity to the source of its existence, nature and purpose, that uncreated Light of God in all his burning righteousness.

The giving of the law is the regard of the Creator for the object of his love, his creature in the contingent relation of its creaturely dimension to him, directing humanity, in a way that its existence could tolerate, to the ground of its proper being and quality in his own Being.

But the temptation to Israel was to regard the law as an

end in itself. The medium of God's protective and interpreting love and concern for creaturely being was manipulated
into a justification of that being. That which protected crea-
tureliness from the blinding brightness and burning of uncreated Light dispelling and consuming all that was not in
correspondence to its nature, was subsumed by human self-
perception generating its own light from the supposed autonomy of its reason, as the means to justify itself. The law no
longer was regarded as paradeigmatic, pointing beyond itself
to the ground of the propriety of human existence in the
Creator, but as a means of exhibiting and illuminating an all
too human piety engendered by self-justification through
that supposed light of self-reasoning. The creature hid
behind the law from the Light of its Creator.

To thus wrest the law from its matrix in the light-ordered
harmony of the totality of creation by the uncreated Light of
the Creator, was to regard the law as Israel's possession for
itself alone and, as a result, to change the perception of
Israel's role within humanity and creation. No longer was
Israel the chosen mirror of God in which the condition of
humanity and the results of its faithfulness and its folly over
against the holiness of God in the light of the Revelation and
Presence of God was reflected to all peoples, that they may
see and believe, but the law became a means of divisiveness
which separated Israel in its pride from all other people. This
is the burden of the apostolic complaint in seeking to interpret the true role of Israel as the womb out of which the
incarnation was brought.

When the fulfilment of the law, that incarnation to which
the law pointed, came – humanity in actual union with that
uncreated Light as the Word of God – this was not perceived
by those who regarded the law as having a different role and
function. The constant and insistent attempts to view our
Lord as being merely another man, and therefore under the
law – *is this not Joseph the carpenter's son? whom do you
make yourself?* and the accusation *you as a man have made
yourself God* – are the attempts to hide again from the Light
which pressed in and brought its scrutiny to bear on their
concealment of themselves behind the law.

Our Lord's own observation with regard to the Pharisees

and Scribes and their piety about the light of the eye being
dark, and that is darkness indeed, is a comment on their
adumbration of the law out of its proper function as light
witnessing to the nature and requirements of uncreated
Light, God in his righteousness. In the same vein, there
is more than time-of-day observation to the description
applied by St John to the beginning of the sequence of our
Lord's betrayal by Judas: *and Judas went out; and it was
night.*

Behind this lie two factors. The first is that when God is
described as 'unapproachable Light', or as 'dwelling in Light
inaccessible', and the Word of God as 'Light', he is being
described as mystery. It is the human inclination to delight in
mystery, but only as that which titillates in the challenge it
proffers for its solution. Mystery which remains mystery is
not, in the last resort, tolerated by our curiosity.

So Lancelot Andrewes' observations, preaching on the text
*And without controversie, great is the Mysterie of Godliness,
which is, GOD is manifested in the flesh ... I Timothy,
chapter III, verse XVI*[1]:

> And even to this day (saith Divinitie), doth the Tree of knowl-
> edge still worke in the sonnes of Eve; we still reckon the
> attaining of knowledge, a thing to be desired, and, bee it
> good, or evil, we love to be knowing, all the sort of us.
> Knowing: but, what? Not, such things as everyone knoweth,
> that goeth by the way; vulgar and triviall. Tush, those are
> nothing. But metaphysickes, that are the Arcana of
> Philosophie; Mysteries, that are the secrets of Divinitie; such,
> as few besides are admitted to: Those be the things we desire
> to know. We see it, in the Bethshemites; they longed to be
> prying into the Arke of God: They were Heathen, we see it in
> the People of GOD too: they pressed too neare the Mount:
> Railes were faine to be sett, to keep them backe. It is, because
> it is held a point of a deepe wit, to search out secrets: as in
> Joseph ... all desire to be in credit ...
> Of God, the Prophet Esay saith (chapter XLV, ver. XV) *Vere
> Deus absconditus es tu:* God is, of himselfe, a Mysterie, and
> hidden; and (that which is strange) hidden with light, which
> will make any eyes past looking on Him. But, a hidden God
> our nature did not endure. Will you heare them speake it
> plainely? *Fac nobis Deos,* Make us Visible Gods, who may go
> before us, and we see them. Mysticall, invisible Gods we

cannot skill of. This we would have; God to be manifested. Why then, God is manifested.

Andrewes goes on to point out that the incarnation, the manifestation of God, does not dissolve the mystery of God. God remains God, but is born in the flesh. This only compounds the mystery of God, for, as he has said already:

> And marke first, that it is not *aliquid Dei*, but *Deus*; not any thing divine, or of God, but God himselfe. Diverse things, diverse invisible things of God had beene formerly made manifest ... But, this is; that, not the things of God, but Gods owne selfe: not the απαυγασμαλα, the beames of His brightnesse; but, the very Character of His substance, the very Nature and Person of God. This, is a great Mystery.

That God in all his Godness should be manifested in the flesh, which is as dust, heightened the mystery:

> There being then (as Abraham said to him (*Luke XVI*) γασμα μεγα, so great a gulfe, so huge a space, so infinite a distance betweene those two, betweene God, and dust; God, and Hay; God, and Corruption, as no comming of one at the other ...
>
> In what flesh? What, in the pride and beauty of our Nature? No: but, in the most disgracefull estate of it that might be. And, how manifested? *Ad gloriam*, for His credit or glorie? No, but *ad ignominiam*, to His great contempt and shame. So to have beene manifested, as in the holy Mount, (His face, as the Sun, His garments as lightning; betweene Moses and Elias, in all glorie, and glorious manner): This had not beene so great an impeachment. Was that the manner? No: But how? In clouts, in a stable, in a manger. The GOD, whom the heavens, and the heaven of heavens cannot contain, in a little Childs flesh not a spanne long ... So to day: but after, much worse. To day, in the flesh of a poor Babe crying in the Cratch, in *medio animalium*: After, in the rent and torne flesh of a condemned person, hanging on the Crosse, in *media latronum*, in the midst of other manner of persons, than Moses and Elias; That, men even hid their faces at him; not, for the brightnesse of His glorie, but for sorrow and shame. Call you this manifesting? Nay, well doth the Apostle call it, the Veile of his flesh; as whereby he was rather obscured, than in any way set forth; yea, eclipsed, in all the darkest points of it. Verily, the condition of the flesh was more than the flesh it selfe: and the manner

of the manifestation, farre more, than the manifestation it selfe was. Both still make the Mysterie greater and greater.

Andrewes concludes that what is manifested is the love of God. God is himself made flesh, but the mystery of God is maintained and not dissolved, heightened and not compromized, by the incarnation. What does become clear in the union of these two opposites, God and man, divinity and corruption, the Infinite and the finite, is that God is love to do this.

> ... when wee have done and said all that ever we can, if we had all Mysteries, and no love, The Apostle tells us, it is nothing. We can have no Mysterie, except Love be manifest. So it is. Two severall times doth the Apostle tell us. 1 (Tit.11) *apparuit Gratia*: 2 (Tit.111) *apparuit amor erga homines*. At the opening of this mysterie, there appeared the 1 Grace of GOD, and the 2 Love of GOD toward mankinde. *Velatio Deitatis, revelatio charitatis*: As manifest as GOD was in the flesh, so manifest was His love unto flesh ... So we have GOD manifested in the flesh, *Deus charitas*: for, if ever He were Love, or shewed it; in this, He was it, and shewed it both. GOD, (that is Love), was manifested in the flesh

What may be obvious to us in the incarnation is the love of God: what can never be obvious is the actual Person of God in all the Majesty of his Godness. That is there, but it is hid from our eyes. The mystery is not resolved or dissolved. The *Deus absconditus*, the hidden God, is revealed precisely as the hidden God who is love and of love towards creation to so involve his very Being in union with the flesh.

Mystery is an affront to our reasoning, for it questions it, and holds it in question. And this the incarnation, supremely, does. It is round the incarnation that all the historic (and present) heresies devised as explanations of mystery primarily gather. Even aberrations concerning the Trinity are in the first resort Chistological deviations. The mystery of uncreated Light, with which we cannot cope, in the dimension of created light, with which we can cope, is ripe, as it were, for what Lancelot Andrewes regarded as hands grasping for knowledge to pluck and consume.

We prefer to reduce the mystery of uncreated Light into the dimension of created light of our existence and reason, for we then can understand and manipulate. We would rather not engage with *fides quarens intellectum*, preferring the controlling, inward, compounding dialectic of our own reasoning, unencumbered and untroubled by the tutelage of the light of objective verities save as obliquely and superficially related to us. For these illumined and enlightening verities can only point to themselves as they are and what they are in the context of that which questions all ways of seeking truth by the solipsism of introverted human understanding, and all supposed truths so gleaned.

The second factor is our readiness to conceptualise. This, of course, is hand in hand with the first factor, our intolerance of that which in its very nature is mystery and remains, in consistency with itself, mystery. It is easier to deal with mystery as a concept, and thus bring it under our controlling thought processes. We prefer to reject Anselm's concept which is valid because it is directed to, and lies within the actuality of, the relation between living Creator and living creature, that God is *that more than which nothing greater can be thought ... even that which is greater than it is possible to think about.* We would rather operate with the reasoning of self-kindled light, and with questioning rather than be questioned, with forming a concept rather than let the mind by reformed against, and by, that which cannot be conceptualized.

In much the same manner as Israel with the law, it is possible to conceptualize the humanity of Christ, treating him as the highest instance of what we already have determined is of value. This means that we sunder Christ, removing his humanity from the union with the Word in which union alone it is given being. Such attempts are a conjectural quest for the 'historical' Jesus. To remove the humanity thus is to attempt to perceive created light as self-producing and unrelated to uncreated Light.

Stripping to what is deemed to be his 'bare humanity', this presentation of Jesus is as a kaleidoscope superficially viewed. All that is seen to lie there is only a jumble of shapes and colours with nothing discernible but disjointed array and riot. What is necessary is that the kaleidoscope be shaken and applied to the eye in a way which allows the structure, ordered in accordance with the principles of the behaviour of light, to operate as it was designed to do. In the focus of this rightness of perception, intriguing, ordered, symmetrical and harmonious patterns may be observed. This is not something imposed artificially from without upon the coloured shapes of the instrument. They have been placed there for this very purpose, and so they belong inherently to this context.

So it is with the humanity, the acts and the sayings of Jesus. Isolated, they are contradictory, enigmatic, with no apparent cohesion or co-ordination. But when, by faith seeking understanding, they are shaken and perceived as that which is the human existence, the words and actions of the Word through the light of resurrection and ascension, there is disclosed their own dynamic, consistent, co-ordinated significant structure and meaning.

And so it is with light. If creation is viewed only in terms of three-dimensional understanding, then all that can be obvious is a bewildering disarray of objects and events in the unrelated chaos of isolated individuality. But appreciating them as light-created, light-sustained and light-ordered, the marvel of created order begins to unfold and take shape, pointing in its unitary harmony to that which is the Source and Determiner of all created light and therefore of all created existence, the Ground of all rationality and intelligibility. To view all things mundanely as the material accidents of time and space, is to interpret merely mechanically, and to disparage and demean unimaginatively the rationality and integrity of the created entities as they really are in themselves in their relation to all else and as they are grounded for their intelligibility on the Rationality of the Creator.

The words of Jesus, if likewise only understood as statements concerned with three-dimensional truths uttered by one who is solely, autonomously human, reduce our Lord to the status of yet another purveyor of yet another philosophy (and a rather incoherent, muddled philosopher at that, with an inconsistency about what, by the same three-dimensional standards of interpretation, are regarded as the categories of 'past', 'present' and 'future', and with a mythological understanding of 'space' and 'place').

But such abstractions fall under the compulsion of the Self-disclosure of the Word made flesh, and the existence of Jesus, his words and his acts, are seen in the dynamic coherence of the incarnation of God, grounded as the genuinely human existence, words and acts of the Word.

This is not to say that all historico/critical approaches to the gospel are to be dismissed. Far from it. But they must not be construed either as understanding seeking faith or as ends in themselves. If the former, then human understanding is accredited with an autonomous status and ability, and assumes the role of judge and arbiter of all, even of God. Faith becomes a nebulous mythology added as speculative and experimental colour to understanding. If the latter, then theology can become only as obsolete as the parallel positivist approach in science, with its disastrous splitting of empirical and theological elements. This causes a theology with such a dualistic outlook to be left behind in the purpose and achievement of intellectual endeavour, being lamentably unfavourable in comparison to the unitary view of the universe opening out in post-Einsteinian thought, and discredited by that thought. It is small wonder that theology is often conceived to be irrelevant and intellectually suspect.

We may speak, on the basis of long precedence, of the existence of the humanity of Christ as that of ανυποστασις and ενυποστασις, 'anhupostasis' and 'enhupostasis'. The first means that the humanity of Christ has no existence outwith its union with the Word. It does not exist independently and of itself. The second indicates that it does have existence, is genuine in its humanity, within the union with the Word. To sunder the humanity from the Word, to cut the union of the Word with the flesh, is not to discover the 'reality' of the humanity, but to deny it its very mode of existence whereby it is *that* humanity, and to give it existence only as the creature of the analytically reductive mind of the biblical critic. The humanity of Christ is therefore only to be understood in context of the hypostatic union.

It is perhaps a comment on how our Lord confronts us as who he is in himself as the Word made flesh, when he himself points out (John VIII:43) that if we cannot understand what he says in earthly terms (λαλια, *lalia*), it is because we cannot, or will not, understand his λογος (*logos*). That is, the light of Christ's words and his humanity can only be grasped properly as they are seen as expressions of the creaturely light of the uncreated Light who personally confronts us in all his Godness being the Word of God.

But there is another level of biblical statement which is contingent to and from this level of the relation between λαλια and λογος, unique in Jesus Christ. He is what he images. He is the uncreated Light to which the light of his words bears witness. His words are the human expressions of the Word, unconfused but inseparable from that Word in the person of Christ. These other biblical statements, unlike his words, are not ontologically related to the Word of God. They are not the flesh, nor the expression of the flesh, of the Word. They may be called 'The Word of God', but only as second hand, as it were. The bible did not become incarnate. Its significance and authority is that it is the paradeigmatic witness to the incarnate One – hence, as we have noted already, he is the σκοπος, the scope, of scripture.

Biblical statements point beyond themselves to the Word made flesh as their goal, their horizon, their true content. In this paradeigmatic nature lies their integrity and their role. There is neither a confusion of word with Word, nor a separation of word from Word, no 'fundamentalist', or rather 'literalist', approach, no dragging down into, and subsuming by, some vaunted autonomy of human critical reason.

As with the 'historical Jesus', so with bible, so with church. These can become institutions divinized, on the one hand, or only mythologically or tangentially related to the truth of God on the other. They can all become conceptualized means of hiding from the hiddenness of God as it confronts us in all the blazing majesty of uncreated Light set before us in the Word made flesh in a way that we can, through faith, come to understanding that this very hiddenness is our Source and Ground and Fulfilment of all things.

We may see this paralleled too in the nature and role of created light. Created light is not uncreated Light. It has its own created rationality, indeed, it is created rationality, but this it holds not autonomously or inherently, but contingently from God. It has this in this relation to uncreated Light, on whom it depends for its beginning, its constancy and its fundamental and completing role in creation. This is its contingency *to* uncreated Light. Its integrity is its contingency; its created nature and rationality accomplishes its role in creation. This is its contingency *from* uncreated Light.

Unless this contingent relation is held, the danger is that the light of reasoning becomes the authority by which all things are judged, and all things confined to all that that reasoning can fit in to its capacities. We then come back to the old error that we can only believe what we understand. It is this which is behind the attempt to arrive at the 'historical Jesus', and as such it may be seen to be a theological attempt to hide from the hiddenness of God, the implications and demands of which being set before us in the incarnation on that hidden God's own terms, for those who have eyes to see that the humanity of Christ is the humanity of uncreated Light, and ears to hear that his words are the words of the Word.

Christ is that unique union between uncreated Light and created light, Word and word, Creator and creature, God and man. He is the hidden God coming out of his unknow-able-ness, so that we may know him as the God who is beyond all created being and the comprehension of creatures, yet makes himself open to them. In Christ our humanity, and our knowing, is opened out to the existence of this hidden God, so that our true life is hid with him in God.

The severing of the humanity of Jesus from its union with the Word allows it, as a concept, to be brought within the control of interpretation merely within the created order. It becomes a 'truth' in the midst of other 'truths', on the same level as, and competing on equal terms with, them. It also results, as the false cognisance of the significance of law and the subsequent misuse of the law did, in Christ as the agent of divisiveness. For the light of his 'truth' so separated from the Truth of uncreated Light, becomes the justification for every human self-perception. That this dismembered Christ is so used is evident from the way in which totally opposed political, cultural and sociological concerns can claim the possession of him as a true relic giving the authority of religious support and validity to their claims.

Christ is thus conceptualized and brought within the dictating and controlling relatives both of the mind of the individual and within the respective collective aspirations within the divisions of humanity.

Even if some sort of relation of the humanity of Jesus to divinity is asserted, all too often that divinity is not the hidden, judging and overwhelming uncreated divinity of the God who dwells in Light unapproachable. It is rather a projection of humanity determined values into their highest instance, by which projection it is assumed that deification is accorded, and therefore still within the created dimension. By such conceptualization, Arianism is brought up to date and flourishes. The uncreated Word is made a creature, an idol either of a vapid universalism of vague amicability towards all, or of sectarian or categorized interests of an exclusive nature.

It is of interest that there is a scientific parallel to this. Paul Davies and John Gribbin (*The Matter Myth*),[2] note that there is a tendency for science to be looked upon merely as a procedure and distorted and manipulated by way of adapting it to certain preconceived doctrines. Hence the rise of 'creation science', 'feminist science', and all the rest. There is, these authors declare, of course only science, which deals with truth not dogma. This truth may well have its limitations, and therefore does not sate those who are bent on embracing and possessing the ultimate truth.

It seems to me that they have already decided what the ultimate truth is, namely the causes or 'philosophies' which they have espoused, and that, motivated by their own ends, regard science as merely conceptual, and thus exploitable for those ulterior objectives.

The same truth in theology. We have seen a rush of 'liberation theology', 'feminist theology', 'green theology' and as many others, no doubt, as the fragmentation of human interests dictates. No doubt some of these concerns have a valid voice among all the relatives of the created order, and equally no doubt, theology has not addressed, as it must (since the created order is the arena of the Word made flesh) the issues so raised. But there is only theology, and it can only address itself to those issues out of the context of its integrity

in relation to the Word made flesh as that Truth is in itself.
That Truth cannot be conceptualized and made to serve
supposedly higher ends, whether these ends are other than
that truth or confused with it. For the Truth of God, to
appeal to Anselm again, is *that than which nothing greater
can be thought*.

Such attempts to relativize truth are to distort the nature of
created light, capture and confine its reflections and mode of
enlightenment, and to accredit that distortion and enlightenment with ultimate validity. So we hide behind the shield of
our conceptions from the Truth of uncreated Light. And,
perhaps, these conceptions are the result of our impatience
with the hiddenness of uncreated Light, and we wish to move
faster than that Light, the necessary waiting of faith seeking
understanding being forsaken and a new and more immediate type of understanding less rigorously available,
embraced.

But what does it mean to be exposed to uncreated Light,
and its judging, overwhelming nature – and, as it is hidden,
where are we exposed to it? Anselm, again, poses much the
same dilemma through the *Proslogion*, but it is in his later
Cur Deus Homo? and its summary in his *Meditation on
Human Redemption* that the full force of his Christocentric
thought is brought to bear on that question.

The 'obscurism' of uncreated Light, the hiddenness of
God, is set forth in the incarnation. It is there that God
stands as man before us in Christ, in all his Godness. The
hiddenness of God is there revealed – but not dissolved. That
is the sum of Anselm's answer to his question *Cur Deus
Homo?* And lies behind his observation:

> In all this, divine nature was not abased, but human nature
> was not made any less, but mankind was mercifully helped.[3]

But this *helped* is through the disclosure in the light of Christ
as to the darkness of human nature, for what is also revealed,
apart from the Lordship of God confronting us as Mystery, is
the hiddenness of human nature as it is before God:

> Weigh up what he was to you, what he did for you ... Think
> what he was to you ... Look into your need ... You were in
> darkness ... You were without any help ... Think and be fear-

> ful ... Lord Jesus Christ, thus did I stand, neither asking nor
> surmizing, when as the sun you gave me light, and exposed to
> me my estate ... I was in darkness, knowing not of myself ...
> When I was destitute of help, you illuminated me and showed
> me what I was.[4]

In this Mystery, all mysteries are revealed – as mysteries and
not admitting to solution by analytical concepts or any other
devising of human endeavour and activity. The mystery of
human alienation from the Source which gives its being beginning, continuance and purpose is exposed as darkness, the
hiding of humanity from the Hiddenness of God. And here,
as he searched for Adam in the garden so he searches for
humanity in Christ to hold and ever embrace it to himself, in
which embrace is its existence and rightness of existence.

This refusal to face and acknowledge the mystery of God
as it is in Christ, and instead seek our own solutions is well
set out in Francis Thompson's *The Hound of Heaven*.

> I fled Him, down the nights and down the days;
> I fled Him, down the arches of the years;
> I fled Him, down the labyrinthine ways
> Of my own mind; and in the mist of tears
> I hid from Him, and under running laughter.
> Up vistaed hopes I sped;
> And shot precipitated
> Adown Titanic gloom of chasmed fears,
> From those strong feet that followed, followed after.
>
> But with unhurrying chase
> And unperturbèd pace,
> Deliberate speed, majestic instancy,
> They beat – and a Voice beat
> More instant than the Feet –
> 'All things betray thee, who betrayest Me.'

The mystery of God made man, the mystery of the incarnation, is, first and foremost, the mystery of the Holy and
Undivided Trinity. The 'how' of this mystery cannot be
answered, nor it, however we seek to change it, explained
away. Nor will it vanish in our hiding from it, but will
compel and press in to our thoughts and existences. We have
to acknowledge, in all rationality, the unanswerable 'how',
and rest content with it on its own terms.

Indeed, the 'how', the το δε πως, of God should not be asked, for this is irrational, as Irenaeus in his own way, and Basil the Great, Gregory of Nyssa and Athanasius make abundantly clear.

It is because the 'how' has been answered already and secretly, and God defined, that some misconstruings of the incarnation occur – Nestorianism, with its division between a divine nature so idealized that it could not possibly take sordid humanity into union with itself, but only be in loose conjunction with it; Apollinarianism with its replacement of the human soul or mind with the divine Logos; Arianism with its reduction of the Word into creaturely status and a resultant incarnation as a union of two qualitatively similar entities – these, and many more, by-passing the essential mystery of the incarnation in asking 'how?' and answering by conceptualizing the divinity, the humanity and the mode of union.

Behind all such attempts is the ever-tempting assertion of the autonomy of the human mind which clings to the twofold idea that what it cannot understand cannot be known and what cannot be known must be irrational, and, as that there is separation between Creator and the creature, the former can only be known by the latter in the projection of its understanding. This became extreme in the case of Arianism, for though it may have been claimed that the Word gives us an understanding of God, since the Word is but a creature, albeit the highest, best and most glorious, this means that what he imparts to us is grounded not on the nature and reality of God, but on humanity's own ability in mental perception. The Word merely is an expression of a 'gnosis', a knowledge which cannot be attained in any other way, but which apart from its confinement to the initiated is no different from any other human attempt to explain things ultimate. That Arianism sprang from the fertile imagination of gnosticism as a general tendency is all too clear, at least from Athanasius's criticism of it.

The biblical witness as to the hiddenness of God speaks of the cloud which surrounds God. It also speaks of God wrapping himself in light as though with a garment. T. F. Torrance, in commenting in the context of St John of the Cross's observations on this, writes[5]:

God is unapproachable because of the sheer invisibility of his uncreated Light, but that invisibility, unlike the invisibility of created light, is to be traced to the transcendence of his Light over our finite capabilities. The higher and the more sublime the divine Light, the more inaccessible, the 'darker' it is to our intellect. It is thus the excess of divine Light over created light which, so to speak, puts God 'in the dark' for us, while the thickness of that darkness is in proportion to the infinite excess of his Light over ours. In Biblical language, by covering himself with Light as with a garment, God shrouds himself in a 'dark cloud' through which our minds cannot penetrate.

It is this God, who infinitely transcends all that we can think or say about him, who has become incarnate. Does this mean that the revelation of God, which the incarnation is, is a negation of the possibility of human knowledge about him – that the Word stands before us in our midst simply as God's 'No!'? God does not cease to be God at the incarnation; he remains constant to himself as he ever was and ever will be. He does not abdicate his nature as God, and therefore remains the hidden God, Lord over our thoughts and statements. But God's 'No!' is but a facet of his 'Yes!' The interplay of this 'No' and 'Yes', not as an opposing dialectic of opposites, is worked out in the life of Jesus Christ, who is not only the Way to the Father, but by that very fact precludes any other way. He is both the Light and the dispeller of the darkness of humanity's alienation from the Source and Ground in the uncreated Light of God.

Nowhere is the 'No!' so loud than in the cry of dereliction on the cross, *My God, my God, why hast thou forsaken me?* That is the cry of the Word made flesh issuing out of the depth of humanity's existence. It is not without significance that in the biblical narrative, all creation shudders at this 'No!' and the sun's light is eclipsed. The great and final issue between God and humanity is wrought out here, where the darkness seems to eclipse the Light of the world, and where better should it be so decided than the place which the Word has made for himself amidst and with humanity?

But that darkness does not extinguish the Light. For the darkness which God is is not as this darkness into which Christ descends at death. It is far greater than it for it is qual-

itatively different. It is the Darkness of his uncreated Light
which dissolves the darkness of creation, because his blinding Darkness is all that is contrary to, and opposed to, our
self-darkness, his Hiddenness the counter to, and Revealer
of, our self-cloaked secrecy. His Light is all that in its radi-
ancy makes of none effect the light that, Promethean-like, we
think to have seized from divinity, but which we have
kindled for ourselves by our supposition that we can see for
ourselves, because our rightful light, whereby we see, stand
upright, walk with dignity and move with purpose, can only
be inflamed from his Light, the Source of all light.

His Light is to us both blinding and illuminating; his 'Yes!'
contains his 'No!' and his 'No!' his 'Yes!' And that is how it
must be if he is God. Revelation does not mean that all is
made easily, automatically and abundantly clear so there is
no more mystery. It means that bestowing of faith in the God
who is that than which no greater can be thought, even that
more than which it is not possible to think. The Self-revelation of God in Jesus Christ is given in its fullness, for
what God eternally is in himself, he is towards us in Jesus
Christ.

But that fulness is more than we can think or compass
within our thoughts. It is not just faith, for that would be
blind, but faith seeking understanding which we are given.
That revelation is given and accommodated to the capacities
of our understanding, but we perceive our understanding to
be by way of faith welling from the unfathomable depth, and
kindled from the unapproachable Light, of God's Being, so
that our understanding by faith is led into the mystery of that
Profundity and enlightened by that Majesty – until that day
when all is made plain and we see face to face. This is the
significance of the Holy Spirit poured out by our Lord leading us into all truth.

In all the acts and sayings of Jesus there is lodged a 'Yes'
and a 'No'. Indeed this is so of his very Person. Simultaneously, his words are gracious, yet are hard sayings; his
acts are of healing yet also of judgement. The sign of the
incarnation itself contains within it a further sign which
makes it clear that the male, Joseph, is pushed aside – the
sign that what is brought forth, while it is for humanity's

sake, is not by man's establishing. Humanity is affirmed in God's assumption of it, his 'Yes!' to it, but this affirmation is on his terms, his 'No!' to all else which thinks it can assert humanity's status and define its dignity. God disables in order that he may enable rightly.

It is unfortunate that sometimes his 'Yes!' only is heard, and therefore not heard rightly. Jesus is made user-friendly, a superficial parody of Christianity. Sometimes only the 'No!' has been heard, and therefore not heard appropriately, a joyless disparagement of humanity. God's 'Yes!' of his 'No!' and the 'No!' of his 'Yes!', the hiddenness of his revelation and the revelation of his hiddenness, the Mystery which he is, is served by neither attitude.

The Spirit, in leading us into all truth, takes the things of Christ and unfolds them, creating faith, seeking understanding and progressing in more understanding. As with the Word, the Spirit is also, in biblical imagery and the theological exposition of the early Church, spoken of in terms of Light. Thus Basil the Great, for example[6]:

> And when, by means of the power which enlightens us, we fix our eyes on the beauty of the image of the invisible God, and through the image are led up to the supreme beauty of the spectacle of the Archetype, then, I perceive, is with us inseparably the Spirit of knowledge, in Himself bestowing upon them that love the vision of the truth the power of beholding the image, not making the exhibition from without, but in Himself leading on to the full knowledge ... As it is written 'in thy light we see light', namely by the illumination of the Spirit, 'the true light which lighteth every man that cometh into the world'. It results that in Himself He shows the glory of the Only begotten, and on true worshippers He in Himself bestows the knowledge of God.

Here the Spirit is regarded as Self-effacing. He does not show anything of himself; he is as invisible light. His role as this invisible Light of God is to show Jesus Christ as the uncreated Light and Word made flesh, and lighten up faith by reflecting the knowledge of God as seen in the face of Jesus Christ. The Spirit is not another Light in addition to the Light of the Word; in his shining he is that Light of the Word in which the Light of the Father is seen. He cannot be treated in separation from the Word, for he does not shine for his own benefit – hence 'He will not speak of himself ... he shall receive of mine, and shall show it unto you', as our Lord says of the Spirit in promising him as the Spirit of truth to his disciples.

While we will be dealing with the question of the Holy Spirit and Light in the next chapter, suffice it here to point out that the Holy Spirit is himself the Invisible, as the uncreated Light of God, and as an analogy from created light, itself invisible but observable in that which it lights up, so the Spirit lights up, as it were, the knowledge of God in the face of Jesus Christ. This Spirit-imparted knowledge through the Word, it is also to be noted, is not a package of total knowing; rather it is a *leading* into all truth.

Again we have the fact that the Self-revelation of God is not our *comprehension* of God, as though he had given himself up to be explained utterly and finally by us. Rather it is our *apprehension* of God, our being granted to share in the knowledge which he has of himself as he exists as Father and Son, bound in the *vinculum caritatis*, the Holy Spirit – a knowledge in which we progress in the Invisible and Incomprehensible by faith seeking understanding, knowing that faith will only vanish into sight on that day when all is fulfilled and we see God face to face. The obscurism of the Light of God's Revelation in and through and by Word and Spirit will always be before us, unencompassed by the created light of being and our reasoning, eluding our conceptualizing and our descriptive analysis, but leading us by faith to more faith and through faith to understanding part by part and piece by piece, through a glass darkly, and more understanding, until the perfect is come. In its apprehension of God, faith is compelled to confess that we can never comprehend him. 'Do you see yonder light?', John Bunyan depicts Pilgrim as being asked. 'I think so', he says and towards it he goes.

Those who say that they have no doubts whatsoever in their faith and act, in the vein of Lancelot Andrewes' remarks about such, as if they had penetrated the very *Cabbinet* of God, that heaven where *even St Paul; never came*, and who have *God's decrees at their finger tips and can count them* 1,

2, 3, 4, would perhaps profit by pondering the gist of Kierkegaard's comment regarding the 'obscurism' of the light of the knowledge of God: *There are no Christians; only the eternal opportunity to become one.*

9

Light, the Word, the Spirit and Humanity

WE HAVE drawn already the analogy between created light, its inherent invisibility and its sole visibility in its reflection of objects, and the Holy Spirit as invisible, as the hiddenness of God, whose role is to reflect for us the Truth as it is in Christ, the Self-revelation of God. We are concerned, therefore, with the Light of the Word by the selfsame Light of the Spirit creating faith and leading faith to understanding. This the Spirit does by bringing us through the Word made flesh into what Irenaeus called a *community of union* with God. Through the Word made flesh, our being and our knowledge is related to, and anchored in, the Being of God as he is eternally in himself, the Source and Ground and Perfecter of all created being and knowledge. The Holy Spirit is the 'Amen' to 'through Jesus Christ our Lord'.

As with the Word, we are to recognize that the Holy Spirit is God in all his Godness. He is not something about God, or something of God, but 'God of God'. Indeed all that may be said of the Word in his eternal existence internal to the Godhead may be said of the Spirit. The Spirit too is 'Light of Light'. Thus Athanasius:

> Because the Spirit is one, and, moreover, is proper to the Word who is one, he is proper to God and of the one substance (ομοουσιος) with him.[1]

So too Epiphanius:

> When you affirm the ομοουσιον, you declare that the Son is God of God, and that the Holy Spirit is God of the same Godhead.

Gregory of Nazianzen also can say:

> We have so much confidence in the Deity of the Spirit Whom we adore, that we will begin our teaching concerning His

> Godhead by fitting to Him the names that belong to the
> Trinity, even though some persons may think us too bold. The
> Father was the True Light which lighteth every man coming
> into the world. The Son was the True Light which lighteth
> every man coming into the world. The Other Comforter was
> the True Light which lighteth every man coming into the
> world. Was and Was and Was, but Was One Thing. Light
> thrice repeated; but One Light and One God. This was what
> David represented to himself long before when he said, In Thy
> Light shall we see Light. And now we have both seen and
> proclaim concisely and simply the doctrine of God the
> Trinity, comprehending out of Light (the Father), Light (the
> Son), in Light (the Holy Spirit).[2]

The holy spirit is *consubstantial* with the Father and the Son[3]
and

> All that the Father hath, the Son hath also, except the being
> Unbegotten; and all that the Son hath the Spirit hath also,
> except the Generation. And these two matters do not divide
> the Substance, as I understand it, but rather are divisions with
> the Substance.[4]

This Unity which is Triunity is more elaborated in the Fifth
Theological Oration *On the Holy Spirit XIV* again in terms
of light:

> To us there is One God, for the Godhead is One, and all that
> proceedeth from Him is referred to One, though we believe in
> three Persons. For One is not more and another less God; nor
> is One before and another after; nor are They divided in will
> or parted in power; nor can you find here any of the qualities
> of divisible things; but the Godhead is, to speak concisely,
> undivided in separate Persons; and there is one mingling of
> Light, as it were of three suns joined to each other. When we
> look at the Godhead, or the First Cause, or the Monarchia,
> that which we conceive, is One; but when we look at the
> Persons in Whom the Godhead dwells, and at Those Who
> timelessly and with equal glory have their being from the First
> Cause – there are Three Whom we worship.

Gregory of Nazianzen, in common with many of his contemporaries, makes much use of the analogy and illustration of
light to speak of the Holy Spirit. He is very clear, however,
that these illustrations have their inbuilt difficulties and
contradictions when applied as analogies of created things to

that which is uncreated. In speaking of illustrating the Persons of the Trinity in their Unity he warns out of wrestlings of his own thoughts that:

> Again I thought of the sun and a ray and light. But here again there was a fear lest people should get an idea of composition in the Uncompounded Nature, such as there is in the Sun and things that are in the Sun. And in the second place lest we should give Essence to the Father but deny Personality to the Others, and make them only powers of God, existing in Him and not Personal. For neither the ray nor the light is another Sun, but they are only effulgencies from the Sun, and qualities of his essence. And lest we should thus, as far as the illustration goes, attribute both Being and Not-Being to God, which is even more monstrous, I have also heard that someone has suggested an illustration of the following kind. A ray of the Sun flashing upon a wall and trembling with the movement of the moisture which the beam has taken up in mid air, and then, being checked by the hard body [of the wall], has set up a strange quivering. For it quivers with many rapid movements, and is not one rather than it is many, nor yet many rather than one; because by the swiftness of its union and separating it escapes before the eye can see it.
>
> But it is not possible for me to make use even of this; because it is very evident what gives the ray its motion; but there is nothing prior to God which could set Him in motion; for He is Himself the Cause of all things, and He has no prior Cause. And secondly because in this case there is also the suggestion of such things as composition, diffusion, and an unsettled and unstable nature ... none of which we can suppose in the Godhead.[5]

The warning of the eventual impropriety of all created images when applied to God is there. Nevertheless, light is the most appropriate analogy (as evidenced by the many references to it in this wise throughout patristic works), as it is in its swiftness, its constancy, its purity and its precision, that which, in the created order, most closely corresponds to the nature of God as uncreated Light.

The demonstration of the Spirit, however, comes best not from illustrations, but from his own abiding Presence with us.

> Now the Spirit Himself dwells among us, and supplies us with a clearer demonstration of Himself.[6]

The knowledge which the Holy Spirit imparts, the knowledge of the Father through the Word, is adapted by the Spirit to our human capacities. It is not given as the overwhelming and blinding glare of the total knowledge of God. We are permitted in our creaturely status to share in the knowledge which God has of himself but in a manner which neither overwhelms us nor leaves us unprotected from the consuming fire of the Majesty of God as he is in himself. While the Holy Spirit comes to us, and is, in the uncreated Light of all his Godness and relation to the Father and the Son, present with us and with all creation, he comes as diffusion in respect for our creaturely frailty of being. We cannot perceive him himself in the invisibility of his uncreated Light, but we do apprehend his reflecting the knowledge of God as it is revealed in the Word made flesh, and his lifting of us, without disestablishing or dissolving our identity as rational creatures, into that Self-knowledge of God by giving us community of union with God through the Word.

So Basil in his *De Spiritu Sancto*,[7] writing of the operation of the Spirit:

> We are compelled to advance in our thoughts to the highest, and to think of an intelligent essence, in power infinite, its magnitude unlimited, unmeasured by times and ages, generous of its good gifts.

But it is to be noted that this is an *advance*. However, it is clear that wherever the fathers speak in this vein, they are not thinking of knowing piece by piece and part by part as though there the truth of God itself is rationed out and imparted piece by piece and part by part. The fullness of that Truth is there Personally in Word and spirit. It is our apprehending of that Truth which advances in this partial but increasing way, as we perceive in the unfolding before us of its height and depth and breadth, yet knowing that that 'dimension' can never be fathomed by our comprehension's line and lead or captured by its hook. We can know the Creator – but as creatures. As T. F. Torrance remarks[8]:

> That God is ineffable does not mean that he is unintelligible.

The coinherence of the Word and the Spirit is the ground of that knowability. Hence Athanasius[9]:

> What is spoken from God is said through Christ and in the Spirit.

But the work of the Word in being made flesh, and the work of the Spirit in being granted to us, takes stock of human being with all its limitations. This is construed in terms of what has been called the 'royal exchange', that is that 'the Word fits himself to our being that he might fit our being to receive the Spirit'. Again, this does not mean the dissolution of creaturely status, but rather, its opening up to verities beyond the limitations of its natural capacities. Hence our knowledge is sometimes described as a 'leading upwards' into more and more light; it is a *leading* into all truth by the opening out of our receptivity for that which is greater than we can conceive. This is the whole movement of faith seeking understanding.

Iranaeus is the great exponent of this potentiality which is not a natural possession but that which is granted. Here I wish to turn to what he says of the matter of the knowledge of God and the mode and limitations of human knowing, for if it is considered in terms of how Iranaeus sees revelation as that which illuminates and reveals that which it illuminates, this leads us on to recognize that just as light does not only bring revelation but bestows revelation of that to which it brings revelation, then we see that the whole process of God's Self-revelation by Word and Spirit is for the dignity of humanity as a creature under God and not merely the enlightening of its mind, to that which is other than itself. It is a process which involves, as is the natural function of created light, the interaction of existences in the integrity of their totalities.

So I preface this short study of Irenaeus's work on the knowledge of God by this quotation from *Adversus Haereses*.[10]

> To follow the Saviour is to be a partaker of salvation, and to follow light is to receive light. But those who are in light do not themselves illumine the light, but are illumined and revealed by it.

The knowledge of God for Irenaeus is principally the knowledge which God has of himself existing as he does as the Father, the Word and the Spirit. The knowledge we have of God is our sharing in his Self-knowledge; it is not a knowledge which we discover for ourselves. Indeed, we cannot achieve such a knowledge; we may come to it only because God graciously reveals himself in the Word made flesh.

> For the Lord taught us that no man is capable of knowing God, unless he be taught of God; that is, that God cannot be known without God; but that this is the express will of the Father, that God should be known. For they, to whomsoever the Son has revealed Him, shall know God.[11]

That God is his own interpreter, and only he can be, is the maxim applicable to Irenaeus's doctrine of the knowledge of God. The incarnation is that self-interpretation. In the light of the incarnation we are permitting to participate in God's knowledge of himself. There are three bases on which that sharing rests and which makes it both possible and actual.

The first is that what God eternally is in himself, he is towards us in Jesus Christ. The Word made flesh is the eternal Word; there is no disjunction between God as he is and God made man. The Word does not sever his relation with the Father and the Holy Spirit to become incarnate, but remains what he is, eternal, immeasurable and uncreated, in his assumption of the temporal and spatial created dimension of the flesh.

> ... that He is Himself in His own right, beyond all men who ever lived, God, and Lord, and King Eternal, and the Incarnate Word, proclaimed by all the prophets, the Apostles, and by the Spirit Himself, may be seen by all who have attained to even a small portion of the truth.[12]

The second is that this knowledge is accessible to humanity because the flesh and nature which the Word assumed at the incarnation is no different from that which constitutes our humanity; it is the same. It is the common humanity we share as the humanity of Adam. There is no disjunction between what we are and what the Word then became; he did not assume a humanity other than that which is our common lot, experience and circumstance in the 'lump of Adam'.

... nor would the Lord have summed up these things in Himself, unless He Himself had been made flesh and blood after the way of the original formation [of humanity], saving in His own person at the end that which had in the beginning perished in Adam.

But if the Lord became incarnate for any other order of things, and took flesh of any other substance, He has not then summed up human nature in His own person, nor in that case can He be termed flesh ... But now the case stands thus, that the Word has saved that which really was, humanity which had perished, effecting by means of Himself that communion which should be held with it, and seeking out its salvation ... He had Himself, therefore, flesh and blood, recapitulating in Himself not a certain other, but that original handiwork of the Father, seeking out that thing which had perished. And for this cause, the apostle, in the Epistle to the Colossians, says, 'And though ye were formerly alienated, and enemies to His knowledge by evil works, yet now have ye been reconciled in the body of His flesh ...'[13]

These two bases are bound together and validated in their effect by a third – the mode of union between God and man at the incarnation. The humanity of Christ is the human nature and flesh of the Word, and it is so in a real sense. That humanity exists only in its union with the Word. It has no other origin than the fact that it is created specifically as the particular flesh and nature which the Word both creates and assumes. The Word becomes one of his own creatures, and specifically this creature. This humanity has existence in its union with the Word; outside that union it has no being whatsoever. The words of Jesus are the words of the Word, for the tongue of Jesus is the Word's personal organ of human speech. The revelation which this Jesus is, is the revelation of God as his Word in relation to the Father and the Spirit. It is not a revelation through another; it is not knowledge at secondhand; it employs no agent for its proclamation; it is God's Self-revelation.

Thus the Immeasurable becomes measurable, but does not lose his immeasurability; the Invisible becomes visible, but is still not open in all his majesty to human gaze and scrutiny. Becoming man, he remains God; constant in his integrity as God, he gives himself to us but does not give himself up thereby contradicting his existence or even compromising the integrity of his Godness.

This revelation of God accommodating himself to the limitations of our existence and understanding is further developed by Iranaeus through and in its accompanying corollary, the reconciliation of God and humanity. This latter doctrine is expressed in terms of what has been called the 'royal exchange'. God, without ceasing to be God, takes to himself our human being and condition, that our humanity may participate in his divine existence and nature. There is an inhomination of God that there may be a deification of man. This last statement means neither that God is 'turned into' man – 'humanized' with regard to his being as God – nor that humanity is transformed into that which is divine – 'divinized' with regard to that which constitutes it as human. The violence of change in the respective essential natures of God and humanity is not meant here. What is meant is both that God remains God but becomes what he was not before, namely man, and that humanity remains humanity but is permitted to have what it had not before, namely communion with the very inner life and transcendent existence of the Triune God. This, and not any change of human nature as human nature into something what it was and is not, is what is meant by 'deification'.

It is this communion with God, which Irenaeus constantly expresses as a *community of union* between humanity and God, which expresses and validates in our existence, the third basis, the mode of union of the divine and human natures at the incarnation. The Word is made flesh for this end, and he is both the substance of this *community of union* of God and humanity and the way whereby it is established in and for us.

But humanity has this not in a mechanical, magical, or even mystical way. Any of these would swallow up or deny the integrity of its created existence and identity. It communion with God is by grace – the free provision of God of participation in the humanity of the Word made flesh by the operation of the Holy Spirit.

These three bases are combined in Irenaeus's constant emphasis on the inseparability of faith and godliness. Revela-

tion cannot be considered apart from reconciliation, nor reconciliation in disjunction from revelation. This is best summed up in the *Demonstration of the Apostolic Preaching*:

> Now, since man is a living being compounded of soul and
> flesh, he must needs exist by both of these: and whereas from
> both of them offences come, purity of the flesh is the restrain-
> ing abstinence from all shameful things and all unrighteous
> deeds, and purity of the soul is the keeping faith towards God
> entire, neither adding thereto nor diminishing therefrom. For
> godliness is obscured and dulled by the soiling and staining of
> the flesh, and is broken and polluted and no more entire, if
> falsehood enter the soul: but it will keep itself in its beauty
> and measure, when truth is constant in the soul and purity in
> the flesh. For what profit is it to know the truth in words, and
> to pollute the flesh and perform the works of evil? Or what
> profit can purity of the flesh bring, if truth is not in the soul?
> For these rejoice with one another, and are united and allied
> to bring man face to face with God.[14]

This underlines Irenaeus's insistence that the whole person is
saved, body and soul, for both are the created handiwork of
God. The knowledge which we may have of God, therefore,
concerns the totality of the individual. Moral theology, in
other words, is not independent of doctrine, nor doctrine of
Christian practice. For this reason, the sacrament of
baptism looms large and is appealed to as holding a domi-
nant position in the setting out of Iranaeus's theological
methodology in the *Demonstration of the Apostolic
Preaching*. For example:

> ... the baptism of our regeneration proceeds through these
> three points: God the Father bestowing on us regeneration
> through His Son by the Holy Spirit. For as many as carry the
> Spirit of God are led to the Word, that is to the Son; and the
> Son brings them to the Father; and the Father causes them to
> possess incorruption. Without the Spirit it is not possible to
> behold the Word of God, nor without the Son can any draw
> near to the Father; for the knowledge of the Father is the Son,
> and the knowledge of the Son of God is through the Holy
> Spirit; and, according to the good pleasure of the Father, the
> Son ministers and dispenses the Spirit to whomsoever the
> Father wills and as He wills.[15]

It is of noteworthy significance that as a necessary continuing commentary in the greatly concentrated discussion on the nature of faith in the *Demonstration of the Apostolic Preaching*, Irenaeus immediately introduces a statement which is the doctrine of baptism and that this statement is set out primarily in credal terms.

> Now faith occasions this for us; even as the Presbyters, the Apostles' disciples, have handed down to us. First of all it bids us bear in mind that we have received baptism for the remission of sins, in the name of God the Father, and in the name of Jesus Christ, the Son of God, who was incarnate and died and rose again, and in the Holy Spirit of God.[16]

The totality of human being is stamped at baptism, where the revealed truth of God is embodied in human existence. Baptism is our incorporation by the Spirit into *the* embodiment of the truth which God is, the Word made flesh, and thereby our participation in the life of God who, by that Word and through the Spirit, is the God committed to the work of his hands. To know God is to behold God face to face, and it is to this end that the Word assumed our flesh and nature:

> ... for this reason did the Word become the dispenser of the paternal grace for the benefit of men, for whom he made such great dispensations, revealing God indeed to men, but presenting man to God, and preserving at the same time the invisibility of the Father, lest man at any time should become a despiser of God, and that he should always possess something towards which he might advance ... For the glory of God is a living man, and the life of man consists in beholding God.[17]

Baptism is the entrance into a life which moves ever on to the beholding of God at the fulfilment of creation, when the work of the Word is revealed openly. It is the initiation into what Athanasius was later to describe in terms of life lived in correspondence to God.

The life of faith which baptism ushers in is a matter of being *led* into truth. The Spirit is promised in terms of the One who will *lead* into that truth. It is not the bestowal of instant, complete knowledge of God. The incorporation into all that the Word made flesh has once and for all and sufficiently done, is an integration of the baptised into the baptism with which Christ was baptised – his strong, determined moving forward, his setting his face towards his cross and passion, and his total obedience to the will of the Father. This he has achieved on behalf of all; he *ministers the things of men to God*, as he also *ministers the things of God to men*, as Athanasius stresses.

Baptism is the incorporation of us into that active and passive obedience, our being thrown into the crucible where humanity is melted and moulded in Christ as God's humanity. It is to take part in that humanity in which Christ advances (προκοπτω), an advance of which Athanasius could write:[18]

> For men, creatures as they are, are not capable in a certain way of reaching forward and advancing in virtue ... the Apostle said that he 'reached forth' day by day to what was before him ... For each had room for advancing, looking to the step before him ... But the Son of God, who is One and Only, what room had He for reaching forward? For all things advance by looking at Him; and He, being One and Only, is in the Only Father, from Whom again He does not reach forward, but in Him abideth for ever. To men then belongs advance; but the Son of God, since He could not advance, being perfect in the Father, humbled Himself for us, that in His humbling we, on the other hand, might be able to increase ... His humbling is nothing else than His taking our flesh. It was not then the Word, considered as the Word, who advanced; who is perfect from the perfect Father, who needs nothing, nay, brings forward others to an advance; but humanly is He here also said to advance, since advance belongs to man ... And, as the Godhead was more and more revealed, so much more did His grace as man increase before all men.

Athanasius underlines the fact that the taking of flesh in no way impaired *the Father's Light, which is the Son*, the divinity of which is unsullied by the incarnation being in all its fullness in the assumption of the flesh. Rather, that advancing of Christ's humanity in its union with the Word is the *shining forth* more and more of the Godhead.[19] The created light of Christ's humanity in union with uncreated Light, shines more and more as this advance, pointing more and more clearly to it both in its Hiddenness in the darkness of the cross and in its overwhelming majesty in the glory of the resurrection – to it as both the 'No!' and the 'Yes!' of God. But not only is it a matter of the revelation of God to us. In that selfsame light of created light in union with the uncreated Light, we, to whom revelation is given by it, are ourselves revealed to be what we are. *In Thy light we see light* does not only refer in this context to the appreciation of the light of objective truth, but also to the understanding of ourselves in the light of that objective truth.

John Calvin noted[20] that in order to see ourselves as we are and to understand ourselves, we must appreciate that:

> it is evident that man never attains to a true self-knowledge until he have previously contemplated the face of God, and come down after such contemplation to look at himself.

But where else do we contemplate the face of God but in the face of Christ, where *God, who commanded the light to shine out of darkness, hath shined in our hearts, to give the light of the knowledge of the glory of God in the face of Jesus Christ?*[21] We may also note the implied Trinitarian formula here, God the Father who created light, the enlightenment of the Spirit in our hearts witnessing to the knowledge of God in the Word made flesh.

Baptism is our incorporation into all that Christ has done and revealed. As such, it is the beginning of faith seeking understanding, as all that Christ has once and for all and sufficiently done is unfolded as we advance in the advance he undertook for us. In it we learn to interpret the visible, all that we are and all our circumstances and all the created reality around us, in terms of the invisible, believing that we may understand. This is an about turn from that practice of thought which normally obtains – interpreting the invisible in terms of the visible, trying to understand so that we can believe. This latter mode of thought is all too prevalent as the legacy we have in the western world of the long and deeply rooted attitude of phenomenalist thinking.

It is here that we can be assisted in our thinking about this by the analogy of light with its inherent invisibility as the means by which we interpret the observable realities around us, and we ourselves with them. As we appreciate the nature of that light, so we come to an understanding of the observable empirical structures of our world and our being, but only by giving credence to the invisible intelligible structures behind them as the controlling objective realities in which created, rationality resides and from which it springs. So with the God who is uncreated Light, on whom all the rationality of this light-ordered creation depends and which gives it beginning, direction and purpose, and the relation between them found to be made and stated in Jesus Christ, that uncreated Light incarnate in our human existence and its created light, the invisible Light of God and the creaturely reflection of that Light, the Light of God not swallowing up and nullifying that reflection, but affirming it and showing it its identity, purpose and dignity. In faith we are led to that understanding by the Spirit, and find ourselves in the going thereto.

10

Light, the Trinity, Baptism and the Christian Life

GREGORY NAZIANZEN'S *Oration on Holy Baptism* is a most significant discourse on the fundamental theological linking of baptism and light. He delivered this oration on the second day of that Festival known in his day as the *Holy Lights*, the Feast of the Epiphany, AD 381, having preached the first oration of the Feast, the *Oration on the Holy Lights* the previous day. In the east, this Feast commemorated particularly the Baptism of Christ.

Four interwoven and inseparable themes run through both orations, and these are knit together by the theme of light: the Trinity, the incarnation, the baptism of Christ and the sacrament of baptism characterizing the Christian life. This is implicit in the opening sentences of the *Oration on the Holy Lights*:

> Again my Jesus, and a mystery ... a mystery lofty and allied to the Glory above. For the Holy Day of the Lights to which we have come, and which we are celebrating today, has for its origin the Baptism of my Christ, the True Light That lighteneth every man that cometh into the world, and effecteth my purification, and assists that light which we received from the beginning from Him from above, but which we darkened and confused by sin.[1]

It is by listening to *the Voice of God* which sounds by and in the One who says *I am the Light of the world* that we are enlightened. Then comes a significant phrase:

> and let not your faces be ashamed, being signed with the true Light.[2]

... the significance lying in the juxtaposition of *light, face* and *signed* within the context of *the Voice of God*. Light is here related to person and identity, to being, again within the context of the Word of God; it is inextricably conjoined with

143

expressed existence and informing audibility. Gregory Nazianzen is speaking here of the relation of light to person within the created dimension. He also speaks – and only on this basis can speak of that created dimension – of light related to Person within the uncreated Existence of the Triune God. Thus:

> We have so much confidence in the Deity of the Spirit Whom we adore, that we will begin our teaching concerning His Godhead by fitting to Him the Names which belong to the Trinity, even though some persons might think us too bold. The Father was the True Light which lighteneth every man coming into the world. The Son was the True Light which lighteneth every man coming into the world. The Other Comforter was the True Light which lighteneth every man coming into the world. Was and Was and Was, but Was One Thing. Light, thrice repeated; but One Light and One God. This was what David expressed to himself long before when he said, In Thy Light shall we see Light. And now we have both seen and proclaim concisely and simply the doctrine of God the Trinity, comprehending out of light (the Father), Light (the Son), in Light (the Holy Spirit).[3]

My purpose here is not to set out an interpretation of Gregory Nazianzen's Trinitarian doctrine, or an analysis of the distinction between his statements on the subject and those of his fellow Cappadocians. It is to put the proposition that above all it is his employment of light which saves him from the liability of misinterpretation by way of subordinationism which lies in the rather questionable emphasis as expressed by Basil and his brother Gregory of Nyssa that the Father is the Αρχη, that is, *Principle*, of the Trinity. For while Gregory Nazianzen certainly does adopt such phraseology, it is nevertheless tempered with balanced consideration of the other Persons, and his insistence that the Μοναρχια, the Monarchia, the sole principle of Godness, is the Godhead, that is the Unity, and not the Father in his ουσια, his substance or essence, alone. This difference of perception, I would advocate, is because of his constant application of the analogy of light paradeigmatically to the uncreated Light which God is.

So it is that while he can write for example[4] that the three Persons have one nature, namely God, but the ground of their unity is the Father, out of whom and towards whom the subsequent Persons are reckoned.

... yet this is not to be construed as meaning that the ουσια, ousia, the substance or essence of the Father is the ground of unity, for as he points out in *Oration XXIX*,[5] *Father* is not a name for ουσια, but for relation (σχεσις).

Father is not a name either of an essence or of an action ... it is the name of the Relation in which the Father stands to the Son and the Son to the Father.

Light is both the characteristic of the three Persons of the Trinity and of the unity between them.

This I commit unto you to-day; with this I will baptize you and make you grow. This I give you to share, and defend all your life, the One Godhead and Power, found in the Three in Unity, and comprising the Three separately, not unequal in substances or natures, neither increased nor diminished by superiorities or inferiorities; in every respect equal, in every respect the same; just as the beauty and the greatness of the heavens is one; the infinite conjunction of three Infinite Ones, Each God when considered in Himself; as the Father, so the Son, as the Son, so the Holy Spirit; the Three One God when contemplated together; each God because consubstantial; One God because of the Monarchia. No sooner do I conceive of the One than I am illumined by the Splendour of the Three; no sooner do I distinguish Them than I am carried back to the One. When I think of any One of the Three I think of Him as the Whole, and my eyes are filled and the greater part of what I am thinking [that is: about God] escapes me. I cannot grasp the greatness of That One so as to attribute a greater greatness to the Rest. When I contemplate the Three together, I see but one torch, and cannot divide or measure out the Undivided Light.[6]

The unity and diversity of light well suits Gregory Nazianzen's exposition of the doctrine of the Trinity. He, in common with his fellow Cappadocians (Basil, Gregory of Nyssa, Didymus the Blind, Evagrius) refused to apply the quantitative distinction of number to the Persons of the Trinity. The divine Nature shared by the Three is in quality absolutely simple, indivisible substance and cannot be divided into parts. In all this, Gregory perceived that he had to steer a fine course between Arian division and Sabellian confusion regarding the Trinity. Indeed, he again and again mentions both Arianism and Sabellianism as the two heretical extremes which regard Deity on the one hand as a division and on the other as a confusion.[7] This rejection of Arian and Sabellian views he accomplishes partly and importantly by his appeal to light.

> When I speak of God you must be illumined at once by one flash of light and by three. Three in *Individualities* or *Hypostases*, if any prefer so to call them, or persons, for we will not quarrel about names so long as the syllables amount to the same meaning; but One in respect of the Substance – that is the Godhead. For they are divided without division, if I may so say; and they are united in division. For the Godhead is one in three, and the three are one, in whom the Godhead is, or to speak more accurately, Who are the Godhead. Excesses and defects we will omit, neither making the Unity a confusion, nor the division a separation. We would keep equally far from the confusion of Sabellius and from the division of Arius, which are evils diametrically opposed, yet equal in their wickedness. For what need is there heretically to fuse God, or to cut Him up into inequality?[8]

His insistence that the Trinity is not to be treated mathematically is clear in *Oration XXI: On the Great Athanasius: 13*, where he points out that Athanasius was

> aware that to contract the Three Persons to a numerical unity is heretical, and the innovation of Sabellius, who first devised a contraction of Deity; and that to sever the Three Persons by a distinction of nature, is an unnatural mutilation of Deity; he both happily preserved the Unity, which belongs to the Godhead, and religiously taught the Trinity, which refers to Personality, neither confounding the Three Persons in the Unity, nor dividing the substance among the Three Persons, but abiding within the bounds of piety, by avoiding excessive inclination or opposition to either side.

Gregory Nazianzen was aware of the difficulties of terminology used to express the doctrine of the Trinity.

> We use in an orthodox sense the terms one Essence and Three Hypostases, the one to denote the nature of the Godhead, the other, the properties of the Three; the Italians mean the same, but, owing to the scantiness of their vocabulary, and the

poverty of terms, they are unable to distinguish between Essence and Hypostases, and therefore introduce the term Persons, to avoid being understood to assert three Essences. The result, were it not piteous, would be laughable. This slight difference in sound was taken to indicate a difference of faith. Then, Sabellianism was suspected in the doctrine of Three Persons, Arianism in that of Three Hypostases, both being the offspring of a contentious spirit.[9]

It was Athanasius, he declares, who in his care of terminology, saw to it that:

> The Trinity was once more boldly spoken of, and set upon the lampstand, flashing with the brilliant light of the One Godhead into the souls of all.[10]

Gregory, above all his fellow Cappadocians, works out the propriety of the orthodox terms in his appeal to the illustration of light. As is above evidenced from the quotation of *Oration XL On Holy Baptism: XLI*, he is insistent that the Monarchia is the Godhead – not the Father, and that this Monarchia is the one Light which is expressed in three radiants. This Light is indivisible in essence. At the same time, he also warns that care has to be exercised in the application of such illustrations to the Triune God, the propriety of any of them having to be severely and finely tested first. He rejects the illustration of the point from where water flows, the subsequent fountain and river, for though the water produced is one, the difference in the forms of the water would encourage a numerical distinction. He then turns to the possibility of using the sun, a ray and the light produced to see if that is a better analogy.[11]

> But here again there was a fear lest people should get an idea of composition in the Uncompounded Nature, such as there is in the Sun and the things that are in the Sun. And in the second place lest we should give Essence to the Father but deny Personality to the Others and make them only Powers of God existing in Him and not Personal. For neither the ray nor the light is another sun, but they are only effulgences from the Sun, and qualities of His essence. And lest we should thus, as far as the illustration goes, attribute both Being and Not-Being to God, which is even more monstrous.

Light itself, without the appeal to sources of light, rays of light emanating from such sources, and so on, is the only illustration which has some propriety in application to God. This, of course, is because it is the created correspondent to God as uncreated Light. Throughout his works, Gregory Nazianzen appeals to this illustration, and it is to be noted that he does so only with care and with warning as to the limits within which it holds its propriety in application to God.

Stemming from this, he also constantly uses the illustration of a *flash* of light. This allows him implicitly and sometimes explicitly to bring in the safeguard of the inability of the human eye to comprehend and encompass the nature of light so seen. Thus, in applying light to our knowledge of God, he can write, as already quoted above:

> When I speak of God you must be illuminated at once by one flash of light and by three.[12]

The Light which God is is also his Self-knowledge. The uncreated Light is the knowledge the Father has of the Son and the Son of the Father in the bond of divine Love, the Holy Spirit. The knowledge we have of God in his Self-revelation is a sharing in that Self-knowledge.

> God is Light; the highest, the unapproachable, the ineffable, That can neither be conceived in the mind nor uttered with the lips, That giveth life to every reasoning creature ... Himself contemplating and comprehending Himself, and pouring Himself out upon what is external to Him. That Light, I mean, which is contemplated in the Father and the Son and the Holy Spirit, Whose riches is Their unity of nature, and the one outleaping of Their brightness.[13]

Light is thus anchored firmly in the concept of Person. But that concept is not an enclosed image, for Person means *Person-in-relation-to-Person*. The Father is only the Father in relation to the Son and the Son only the Son in relation to the Father and the Spirit only the Spirit in relation to both and both only as they are in relation to the Spirit. Light is both the very ουσια, the ousia, the substance, of God, and the very nature and identity of the υποστασεις, the hypostases, the Persons, being one ουσια, in their relation.

One ousia and three hypostases was the orthodox formula

fixed once and for all at Constantinople in AD 381. To this the Cappadocians fiercely clung, interpreting it in their own way, and among them no one more ably its defender and advocate than Gregory Nazianzen. I would wish to put forward the claim that he does so more adeptly than his fellows because of his constant appeal to the illustration of light.

Out of this analogy he is able, bearing in mind the safeguards on which he insists in the application to the Uncreated of all analogies and illustrations from the created order, to penetrate more clearly into the relations of the Trinity by appreciating light and using it as a pointer in its properties, its behaviour, its primacy, its constancy, and its unity in diversity and diversity in unity, to the ineffable and impenetrable relations of Father, Son and Spirit. Each is distinguished by his peculiar property (ιδιοτης); the distinction most certainly is not a differentiation of substance (ουσια) among them. It is this which marks out each hypostasis or Person, but all are of one ousia or Substance – they are ομοουσιον, homoousion, of one substance.

I would advance the proposition that in Gregory Nazianzen's thought these properties or characteristics are perceived implicitly in terms of Light Begetting, Light Begotten and Light Embracing, and that behind the advocacy of the ομοουσιον lies his awareness that Light is Light and cannot be differentiated in substance, in its essential being.

The Light which God is, is one. The Father, the Son and the Holy Spirit are both in the distinction of their Persons that uncreated Light and in the unity of the Godhead that uncreated Light. But Gregory Nazianzen distinguishes other sorts of light. The uncreated Light of God is the first. This divine Light is other than all other light for it is

> the unapproachable, the ineffable, That can neither be conceived in the mind nor uttered with the lips.[14]

The second is the Angelic light. He does not speculate on angelic existence, expressing an agnosticism in that area. He is concerned to state, however, that that existence is one of light and obedience. That is to say, it is in correspondence and concord with the ineffable Light of God, for the angelic light is

> a kind of outflow of communication of that First Light, draw-
> ing its illumination from its inclination and obedience thereto;
> and I know not whether its illumination is distributed accord-
> ing to the order of its state, or whether its order is due to the
> respective measures of its illumination.[15]

The idea is here tentatively expressed in the second possibility that being is the result of light, and generally Gregory
Nazianzen follows this alternative view of existence in his
other categories of light and existences. This is certainly so in
the matter of divine Light, where God is expressly called
Light. It also holds in his third category of light, namely
humanity itself. Man too is called *light*. This would not have
been a description outwith the common understanding, for it
would be recognizable from the long-standing poetic description of man as light, contemporary to Gregory Nazianzen.
This called humanity *light*, as Gregory notes, because of the
faculty of speech which was its possession. There is a
common understanding, then, that light and rationality are
bound together. But Gregory qualifies that rationality in
Christian terms of those

> who are more like God, and who approach God more nearly
> than others.[16]

That is to say, created rationality is correspondence to the
uncreated Rationality of God, and the light of reasoning and
human existence qualified by its approximation to the uncreated Light which God is. It is thus that he treats the obedience of the angelic existences in terms of the even closer
approximation to that uncreated Light which they enjoy.[17] It
is the beginning of, and progress in, that increasing approximation to God of humanity as created rationality, which is
the significance of baptism and the Christian life. That is not
to say that Gregory Nazianzen is, first, limiting light to rationality in terms of only mental understanding, or, second,
limiting rationality to humanity. He distinguishes yet another
type of light, namely that

> by which the primeval darkness was driven away or pierced.
> It was the first of all the visible creation to be called into exis-

tence; and it irradiates the whole universe, the circling orbit of the stars, and all the heavenly beacon fires.[18]

Creation is typified by light and is thereby a creation of rationality in its order and the exercise, movement, functioning of, and relations within, that order. It is a twofold creation. The first creation is that of the heavenly host, the second the material and visible world. But they are the one creation, accomplished by the Word and the Spirit. Creation, too, has a unity and a diversity.

Its diversity is that it is composed of the heavenly and the earthly. Its unity, for Gregory, again centres round light. While light is the creative principle of both, there is a more specific bond of union and that is man as the creature whose rational mind has a relation to the Light of Truth. He sets it out in his fashion:

The Godhead, the Monarchia of God, is neither greater nor lesser than the Three Persons of the Trinity. It is the Holy of Holies, hidden even from the Seraphim, but is glorified by the thrice repeated 'Holy' which meets in one ascription of the title 'Lord and God'.[19] God is that Goodness who contemplates and knows himself in his Triune existence, but his Goodness is not satisfied with the movement of Self - contemplation alone. Its very nature means that it has to pour itself out beyond itself in order to share this beneficence. And so God, who is the Primary Splendour, conceives in thought those existences which are the angelic and heavenly powers, and brings the conception to fulfilment by his Word and the Spirit perfecting the work. These angelic existences are Secondary Splendours, and, as such, are ministers of the Primary Splendour. We have to note here that as ministers they are qualitatively distinct from God, and, being brought into being as a creative act by Word and Spirit, they are not in Gregory's theology emanations or extensions of the uncreated Light which is God.

Moreover, while he would like to be able to say that they are capable only of good and resistant to any inclination towards evil (which is the disposition of God alone), he cannot. They are illuminated by the first Rays from God (we note that they are not of the quality of the Light which God is, but only *illuminated* by them). It is in this that their splendour holds together. But the one who for his splendour was even called Lucifer, *became and is called Darkness through his pride.*[20]

When this first world of the intelligible world was in good order, God brings into being a second world *material and visible.* This is a *system* of earth and sky and everything within them. Its unity and diversity is a fact of marvel:

> an admirable creation indeed when we look at the fair form of every part, but yet more worthy of admiration when we consider the harmony and unison of the whole, and how each part fits in with every other in fair order, and all with the whole, tending to the perfect completion of the world as a Unit.[21]

With the first world, God brings into being that which is *akin to Himself* (again we note that this is other than God and not an extension or emanation of him). The angelic existences are *akin* to him because they are *intellectual and only to be comprehended by mind.* That is to say, this world which is the *intellectual* world is invisible and intelligible world. With the second, visible and sensible world, he brings into existence that which is *alien* to him. That is to say, God is not material, temporal and spatial. He is Being, and as such the Source and Author of all being in his overflowing Goodness, and therefore is other than and qualitatively beyond created being.[22]

The physical objects which are the parts of this second world also in their own way and in accordance with their natures, fulfil a role as 'ministers' of God, just as those existences of the first world do in correspondence with their nature.

> Mind then and sense, thus distinguished from each other, had remained within their own boundaries, and bore in themselves the magnificence of the Creator-Word, silent praisers and thrilling heralds of His mighty work.[23]

Humanity, for Gregory, stands astride both worlds, the intelligible and the sensible, and in emphasizing this status of human existence, he strongly if implicitly implies that humanity is a unifying principle, a full statement, a quintessential personification, of all the light-founded and light-sustained orders and realities of creation, heavenly and earthly, intelligible and sensible. Humanity, therefore, possesses a unique estate and role in the universe, and this purpose and function is centred on light.

> Mind then, and sense, thus distinguished from each other, had remained within their own boundaries [he is writing here of the creation of heaven and heavenly existences, that is the intelligible world, and the physical creation with all that it is in its temporal and spatial realities as the sensible world], and bore in themselves the magnificence of the Creator Word, silent praisers and thrilling heralds of His mighty work. Not yet was there any mingling of both, nor any mixture of these opposites, tokens of a greater wisdom and generosity in the creation of natures; nor as yet were the whole riches of goodness made known. Now the Creator–Word, determining to exhibit this, and to produce a single living being out of both (the invisible and the visible creation, I mean) fashions Man; and taking a body from already existing matter, and placing in it a Breath taken from Himself (which the Word knew to be an intelligent soul, and the image of God), as a sort of second world, great in littleness, He placed him on the earth, a new Angel, a mingled worshipper, fully initiated into the visible creation, but only partially into the intellectual; king of all upon earth, but subject to the King above; earthly and heavenly; temporal and yet immortal; visible yet intellectual; half-way between greatness and lowliness; in one person combining spirit and flesh; spirit because of the favour bestowed on him, flesh on account of the height to which he had been raised; the one that he might continue to live and glorify his benefactor, the other that he might suffer, and by suffering be put in remembrance, and be corrected if he became proud in his greatness; a living creature, trained here and then moved elsewhere; and to complete the mystery, deified by its inclination to God ... for to this, I think, tends that light of Truth which here we possess but in measure; that we should both see and experience the Splendour of God, which is worthy of Him Who made us, and will dissolve us, and remake us after a loftier fashion.[24]

But this creature, who is the composite of both worlds, disobeyed the commandment given him by God – an injunction which was itself light:

> Light was also the firstborn commandment given to the first-born man ... although the envious darkness crept in and wrought wickedness.[25]

There is here an Irenaean insistence that life is a matter of development towards maturity. The reason for the fall of humanity is that Adam and Eve seize the fruit of the Tree of Knowledge before they are ready to assimilate its benefits. In writing of the creation of humanity, Gregory states:

> This being He placed in Paradise ... to till the immortal plants, by which is meant perhaps the Divine Conceptions, both the simpler and the more perfect; naked in his simplicity ... Also he gave him a Law, as a material for his Free Will to act upon. This Law was a Commandment as to what plants he might partake of, and which one he might not touch. This latter was the Tree of Knowledge; not, however, because it was evil from the beginning when planted; nor was it forbidden because God grudged it to us ... let not the enemies of God wag their tongues in that direction, or imitate the Serpent ... But it would have been good if partaken of at the proper time, for the tree was, according to my theory, Contemplation, upon which it is only safe for those who have reached maturity of habit to enter; but which is not good for those who are still somewhat simple and greedy in their habit; just as solid food is not good for those who are yet tender, and have need of milk ... alas for my weakness! (for that of my first father was mine), he forgot the Commandment which had been given to him; he yielded to the baleful fruit; and for his sin he was banished at once from the tree of life, and from paradise, and from God; and put on the coats of skins, that is, perhaps, the coarser flesh, both mortal and contradictory.[26]

At the end of this section on the Fall, Gregory Nazianzen notes that death is a punishment from God yet is a mercy from God and a gain for man. It is the limitation of evil, for by the death of man evil is denied immortality. That is, as man's forfeit of his immortality is God's circumscription of evil.

One main argument in this recount of the Fall is that humanity was not yet mature enough to taste the fruit of the tree of knowledge. This exactly reflects Irenaeus's observations on the matter of humanity's immaturity at creation:

Now, having made man lord of the earth and all things in it, he secretly appointed him lord also of those who were servants in it [that is, the angels]. They, however, were in their perfection; but the lord, that is, man, was [but] small; for he was a child; and it was necessary that he should grow, and so come to [his] perfection ... But man was a child, not yet having his understanding perfected; wherefore also he was easily led astray by the deceiver.[27]

Lest man should conceive thoughts too high, and be exalted and uplifted, as though he had no lord, because of the authority and freedom granted to him, and so should transgress against his maker God, overpassing his measure, and entertaining selfish imaginings of pride in opposition to God; a law was given to him by God, in order that he might perceive that he had as lord the Lord of all. And he set him certain limitations, so that, if he should keep the commandment of God, he should ever remain as he was, that is to say; immortal; but, if he should not keep it, he should become mortal and be dissolved to earth from whence his formation had been taken.[28]

Some of Irenaeus's distinctive emphases and characteristics of thought and themes (and indeed, terminology) appear in the writings of Gregory Nazianzen. Certainly Irenaeus's manifold idea of the necessity of humanity to progress in the knowledge of God, man being created a child and therefore vulnerable to evil's manipulation, his untimely seizing of knowledge which therefore redounds to his ruin, and the necessity of restoring the way of true enlightenment for humanity, is paralleled as the interpretation of the Fall by Gregory.

It is not surprizing that Gregory was such an avowed opponent of Apollinarianism, for he is insistent that the mind, above all, is at the root of the Fall. In complaining about the folly of pagan Greek belief and the resultant demeaning of human dignity and behaviour, he writes:

Well, let these things be the amusement of the children of the Greeks and of the demons to whom their folly is due, who turn aside the honour of God to themselves ... ever since they drove us away from the Tree of Life, by means of the Tree of Knowledge, unseasonably and improperly imparted to us, and then assailed us as now weaker than before; carrying clean away the mind, which is the ruling power in us, and

> opening a door to the passions ... For this God's Image was
> outraged; and as we did not like to keep the Commandments,
> we were given over to the independence of our error.[29]

His interpretation of the Fall and the way of remedy uses the
argument that the condemnation is the mercy of God: by the
grace of God fear is precipitated in us: the beginning of
wisdom to get wisdom: and it is that fear of God which is the
beginning of Wisdom. Such is the nature of this gracious fear
that it causes us to flee error, be joined to the truth, and to
look at God who is over and beyond creation:

> let us look at and reason upon God and things divine in a
> manner corresponding to this Grace given us ... we must be
> grounded and purified and so to say made light by fear, and
> thus be raised to the height. For where fear is there is keeping
> of commandments; and where there is keeping of command-
> ments there is purifying of the flesh, that cloud which covers
> the soul and suffers it not to see the Divine Ray. And where
> there is purifying there is Illumination; and Illumination is the
> satisfying of desire to those who long for the greatest things, or
> the Greatest Thing, or That Which surpasses all greatness.[30]

But this illumination of humanity comes not by its own
efforts and ingenuities, wit and wisdom. Baptism is the
beginning of that process of illumination, of more and yet
more enlightenment, which is the characteristic and hallmark
of the Christian life. This baptism is in itself the conjoining of
the individual with the Word made flesh, his or her communion with his Person and participation in his saving and
enlightening acts. The natural light of humanity bestowed
upon it at creation is lost in the darkness of self-appointed
delusion and turning from God; this is restored and more
than restored in him who is Light itself. Those baptized are

> fenced by the Trinity ... illumined by Christ.[31]

Catechumens are

> but in the porch of Religion; you must come inside, and cross
> the court, and observe the Holy Things, and look into the
> Holy of Holies, and be in company with the Trinity.[32]

Children of the tenderest years should be brought to baptism –

Have you an infant child? Do not let sin get any opportunity, but let him be sanctified from his childhood; from his very tenderest age let him be consecrated by the Spirit. Fearest thou the Seal on account of the weakness of nature? ... Give your child the Trinity, that great and noble Guard.[33]

Some will say ... what have you to say about those who are still children, and conscious neither of the loss nor of the grace? Are we to baptize them too? Certainly, if any danger presses. For it is better that they should be unconsciously sanctified than that they should depart unsealed and uninitiated. A proof of this is found in the Circumcision on the eighth day, which was a sort of typical seal, and was conferred on children before they had the use of reason.[34]

It must not be construed that Gregory is regulating and confining the baptism of children to those in extremis. One of his purposes in this oration is to persuade people not to delay their baptism until their death bed. He specifically warns that death stands at everyone's hand at every moment, so that baptism should be sought by them and administered to them *seasonably* – that is at every opportunity.

Every time is suitable for your ablution, since any time may be your death.[35]

There is no age nor condition of humanity which is excluded from the sacrament. Here another Irenaean theme is entered upon – the hallowing by the Word in the assumption of the flesh not only of the totality of what we are, but also of all ages and circumstances recapitulated by him. Ireneaus could write that the Word

not despising or evading any condition of humanity ... passed through every age, becoming an infant for infants, thus sanctifying infants; a child for children, thus sanctifying those who are of this age ... a youth for youths ... an old man for old men ... then, at last, He came on to death itself ...[36]

Wherefore also He passed through every stage of life, restoring to all communion with God.[37]

In the same vein, though much expanded and by looking at the matter from the side of human experience and the endeavours of the Christian life out to the experiences and circumstances of the Word made flesh, putting them in the light of that context, Gregory Nazianzen in his Orations on the *Theophany, the Holy Lights* and *Holy Baptism*, sets out, in his own style and use of oratory, the reasons why all sorts and conditions are in company with Christ, that they should be baptized, no excuse availing.

That is why baptism, at any age and for any estate of humanity is *seasonable*.

> With Paul I shout to you with that loud voice, 'Behold now is the accepted time; behold Now is the day of salvation'; and that Now does not point to any one time, but is every present moment ... let every time be to you the definite one for Baptism.[38]

In his Oration XXXVIII *On the Theophany*, he lists the terms of the Christian life as sharing in the endeavours and circumstances of Christ.

> Travel without fault through every stage and faculty of the Life of Christ ... strip off the veil which has covered thee since thy birth.[39]

That Christian life is to the end that

> you may be like lights in the world, a quickening force to all other men; that you may stand as perfect lights besides That great Light, and may learn the mystery of the illumination of Heaven, enlightened by the Trinity more purely and clearly, of Which, even now you are receiving in a measure the One Ray from the One Godhead in Christ Jesus our Lord.[40]

Baptism is our incorporation in Christ. It is both the granting of light and the taking up of that light which is each individual to be constituted in its own propriety in the greater Light of God in Christ. Our light is not swallowed up, made to disappear, and be disanulled, in the greater. On the contrary, it is established and strengthened and affirmed in that Light.

Baptism rests on the incarnation. The assumption of human nature by the Word is expressed in terms of the 'royal exchange' by Gregory Nazianzen. This he does in the Irenaean mode of listing opposites: thus:

> An innovation is made upon nature, and God is made Man. 'He that rideth upon the Heaven of Heavens in the East' of His own glory and Majesty, is glorified in the West of our meanness and lowliness. And the Son of God deigns to

become and be called Son of Man; not changing what He was
(for It is unchangeable); but assuming what He was not (for
He is full of love to man), that the Incomprehensible might be
comprehended ... Therefore the Unmingled is mingled; and
not only is God mingled with birth and Spirit with flesh, and
the Eternal with time, and the Uncircumscribed with measure;
but also Generation with Virginity, and dishonour with Him
who is higher than all honour; He who is impassible with
Suffering, and the Immortal with the corruptible.[41]

Humanity is thus sanctified, and in baptism that sanctifica-
tion is sealed. Again, this is worked out in terms of light. In
discoursing on baptism, he describes it as specially related to
Illumination.

Illumination is the splendour of souls, the conversion of the
life, the question put to the Godward conscience. It is the aid
to our weakness, the renunciation of the flesh, the following
of the Spirit, the fellowship of the Word, the improvement of
the creature, the overwhelming of sin, the participation of
light, the dissolution of darkness. It is the carriage to God, the
dying with Christ, the perfecting of the mind, the bulwark of
Faith, the key of the Kingdom of Heaven, the change of life,
the removal of slavery, the loosing of chains, the remodelling
of the whole man ... Illumination is the greatest and most
magnificent of the Gifts of God ... so is this called Illumination, as being more holy than any other illumination
which we possess.
    And as Christ the Giver of it is called by many various
names, so too is this Gift ... the Gift, the Grace, Baptism,
Unction, Illumination, the Clothing of Immortality, the Laver
of Regeneration, the Seal, and everything that is honourable.
We call it the Gift, because it is given to us in return for nothing on our part; Grace, because it is conferred even on
debtors; Baptism, because sin is buried with it in the water;
Unction, as Priestly and Royal, for such were they who were
anointed; Illumination, because of its splendour; Clothing,
because it hides our shame; the Laver, because it washes us;
the Seal, because it preserves us, and is moreover the indication of Dominion. In it the heavens rejoice; it is glorified by
Angels, because of its kindred splendour. It is the image of the
heavenly bliss. [42]
    Light ... in a special sense is the illumination of Baptism ...
for it contains a great and marvellous sacrament of our
salvation.[43]

This incorporation into Christ by baptism is no easy thing. It is the beginning of a lifelong and arduous struggle. But baptism, by which the Trinity is our defence since in Christ we are baptized into that divine Existence, does not mean that we have arrived, as it were, once and for all impeccable and perfect. It is the means to put evil to flight. Again, the reference is to incorporation into the experiences and existence of Christ:

> If after baptism the persecutor and tempter of the light assail you (for he assailed even the Word of my God through the veil [that is, the humanity of Christ], the hidden light through that which was manifested), you have the means to conquer him ... Say to him, relying on the Seal, 'I am myself the Image of God; I have not yet been cast down from the heavenly Glory, as thou wast through thy pride; I have put on Christ; I have been transformed into Christ by Baptism; worship thou me'. Well do I know that he will depart, defeated and shamed by this; as he did from Christ the first Light, so he will from those illumined by Christ. Such blessings does the laver bestow on those who apprehend it ...[44]

It is significant that Gregory Nazianzen indulges in language and description which almost identifies the baptized with Christ, so insistent is he on the union which is brought about between them by all that Christ is and does in his grace. This is described as *Communion*, and here again there are echoes of Irenaeus's phrase for the relation between God and humanity through Christ – a *community of union*.

> I had a share in the image; I did not keep it; He partakes of my flesh that He may both save the image and make the flesh immortal. He communicates a second Communion far more marvellous than the first, inasmuch as then he imparted the better nature, whereas now Himself partakes of the worse. This is more godlike than the former action, this is loftier in the eyes of all men of understanding.[45]

The progress of the baptized in a community of union with Christ and in the Christian faith, is described by Gregory in terms of *flashes of lightning*. It is not that the faithful are surrounded once and for all in perfect light. They move towards that fulfilment in resurrection, when they are in the presence of uncreated Light. The constant reference to lightning flashes preserves the priority of Light over our comprehension of it. It always precedes us, is above and beyond us. It is more than our sight can bear, and it is elusive for it is given on its own terms and not on our demand for our possession of it. We cannot see the Divine Light in its constant fullness; we may only catch glimpses of it.

In this consists the advance of the Christian life. Again, this is set out by Gregory in terms of light and in the context of the Self-revelation of the Trinity.

> Theology ... here perfection is reached by additions ... The Old Testament proclaimed the Father openly, and the Son more obscurely. The New manifested the Son, and suggested the Deity of the Spirit. Now the Spirit Himself dwells among us, and supplies us with a clearer demonstration of Himself. For it was not safe, when the Godhead of the Father was not yet acknowledged, plainly to proclaim the Son; nor when that of the Son was not yet received to burden us further (if I may use so bold an expression) with the Holy Spirit; lest perhaps people might, like men loaded with food beyond their strength, and presenting eyes as yet too weak to bear it to the sun's light, risk the loss of even that which was within their powers; but by gradual additions, and, as David says, Goings up, and advances and progress from glory to glory, the Light of the Trinity might shine upon the more illuminated ...
>
> You see lights breaking upon us, gradually; and the order of Theology, which it is better for us to keep, neither proclaiming things too suddenly, nor yet keeping them hidden to the end. For the former course would be unscientific, the latter atheistical; and the former would be calculated to startle outsiders, the latter to alienate our own people.[46]

The lightning flash serves a triple purpose as an illustration of gradual illumination in the knowledge of God.[47] Its blinding brilliance suggests the incomprehensibility of God and his glory; we can comprehend part of it and acknowledge it; but its fleeting and overpowering radiance excites our wonder. This is what Anselm was later to draw out as faith seeking understanding of the God who is greater than that which we can think. Through the illumination of faith we are given some understanding, and that in turn provokes more faith and again in turn in that faith more understanding. The parallel with Anselm's thought may be appreciated in this extract:

God always was and always is, and always will be; or rather,
God always Is. For Was and Will Be are fragments of our
time, and of changeable nature. But He is Eternal Being; and
this is the Name he gives Himself when giving the Oracles to
Moses in the Mount. For in Himself He sums up all Being,
having neither beginning in the past nor end in the future ...
like some great Sea of Being, limitless and unbounded, tran-
scending all conception of time and nature, only adumbrated
by the mind, and that very dimly and scantily ... not by His
Essentials but by His Environment, one image being got from
one source and another from another, and combining into
some sort of presentation of the truth, which escapes us
before we have caught it, and takes flight before we have
conceived it, blazing forth upon our master-part, even when
that is cleansed, as the lightning flash, which will not stay its
course, does upon our sight ... in order, as I conceive, by that
part of it which we can comprehend to draw us to itself (for
that which is altogether incomprehensible is outside the
bounds of hope, and not within the compass of endeavour);
and by that part of It which we cannot comprehend to move
our wonder; and as an object of wonder to become more an
object of desire; and purifying to make us like God; so that
we, when we have become like, God may, to use a bold
expression, hold converse with us as God; being united to us,
and known by us; and that perhaps to the same extent as He
already knows those who are known to Him.[48]

Another of his favourite illustrations is that of the *candle* or
the *lamp*. This is applied first and foremost to the humanity
of Christ (e.g. Oration XXXVIII) *On the Theophany*: XIV;
Oration XLV: the Second Oration on Easter: XXVI), then to
John Baptist (e.g. Oration XLV: the Second Oration on
Easter: XXVI): and finally to the individual Christian (e.g.
Oration XL *On Holy Baptism*: LXVI). It is an apt symbol, if
for nothing else, the fact that a candle does not generate its
own light, but requires to be lit from another source.

Let us not walk in the light of our fire, and in the flame which
we have kindled.[49]

Thus the flesh of Christ has not its own existence, but is
given its existence in its union with the uncreated Light, the
Word himself. So too, John Baptist, *the Candle-Forerunner*,
has no significance of his own, but has great place in that he
points to the One who is to come after him. He is not that

Light, but is sent to bear witness of that Light. Equally, both the existence and the faith of the individual is neither a natural possession nor a self-achieved reward. It is a matter of the grace of God, who gives both the light of life and the enlightenment of faith, creating, embracing, sustaining and fulfilling both in the Word and Spirit and relating them in communion with the threefold Light of his Triune Being.

Light, for Gregory, is dynamic, animated and animating. It is inextricably linked with being. In the first instance it refers to the eternal Being of the Triune God, and to the uncreated Light-ordered Existence of Rationality which he is. He refers to various kinds of light,[50] distinguishing between the uncreated Light of God, and created light, in which latter category variations are found differing in form and purpose within creation though not in essence. Light remains light, the only distinction is that between the Light of the Creator and the light of the creature. The unity and diversity of the orders and rationality of existence in the created dimension are dependent upon the Unity and Diversity of the Order and Rationality of the Triune Being of the Creator. Created light, in whatever form it takes, is in a relation of double contingence to that uncreated Light. It is not uncreated Light, but it holds its nature and characteristic as the created correspondent to the uncreated Light. It is therefore, in all its forms, paradeigmatic – constantly pointing to, persuading of and leading towards the Source of all Light and Existence. This is found above all in the Word made flesh, who as the Light of the world enters his creation, giving created light the integrity to be what it is amid the darkness of the alienation of creation hiding in the darkness of the light which humanity has kindled for itself.

It is this latter false light, which is really darkness, against which Gregory Nazianzen warns. The true light is distinguished from this because of its relation to the Light of God. Here we are given not only the test for light but the test for knowledge and truth as well. Truth is that which resides in the integrity of the object of truth and not in the presuppositions and self-regarding ability of the human mind. It is in this presumed capacity of man to determine out of himself what is truth and what is not that the falsity of this self-accredited light lies. This, moreover, is a false dignity and potential which humanity ascribes to itself.

> And as I know of two kinds of fire, so also do I of light. The one is the light of our ruling power directing our steps according to the will of God; the other is a deceitful and meddling one, quite contrary to the true light, though pretending to be that light, that it may cheat us by its appearance. This really is darkness, yet has the appearance of noonday, the high perfection of light. And so I read that passage [Isaiah XVI:3] of those who continually flee in darkness at noonday; for this is really night, and yet is thought to be bright light by those who have been ruined by luxury. For what saith David? 'Night was around me and I knew it not, for I thought that my luxury was enlightenment [a paraphrase of the last part of the Septuagint version of Psalm CXXXIX:11]'. ... that amongst other things we may learn what is the true light, and what the false, and be saved from falling unawares into evil wearing the disguise of good ... Let us be made light, as it was said to the disciples by the Great Light, ye are the light of the world. Let us be made lights in the world, holding forth the Word of Life; that is, let us be made a quickening power to others. Let us lay hold of the Godhead; let us lay hold of the First and Brightest Light. Let us walk towards Him shining ... not in ... the dishonesties of the night.[51]

This true light concerns the totality of human existence:

> Let us cleanse every member, Brethren, let us purify every sense; let nothing in us be imperfect or of our first birth; let us leave nothing unilluminated. Let us enlighten our eyes, that we may look straight on ... Let us be enlightened in our ears; let us be enlightened in our tongue, that we may hearken what the Lord God will speak, and that He may cause us to hear His loving kindness in the morning.[52]

The being of humanity as an existence of true light is directed to where it is grasped by the uncreated Light of God. That is why baptism into Christ is baptism into, and a life directed to, the Trinity.[53]

In all this I have sought to let Gregory Nazianzen speak for himself, as it were, without the interruption of overmuch commentary from me. He is rightly dubbed *the Theologian*, but I would suggest that because there are hardly any of his writings in which the theme of light does not appear, for he so largely appeals to it, that he should be fittingly entitled *the Theologian of Light*. Light and life for him are one, and the created light and life of our existence and of all creation's existence, the way in which the whole universe variously and unitedly lives, moves and has its being, as light-founded and light-sustained order and rationality, is its relation, its community of union through the Word made flesh, the Light of the world, with the uncreated Light of the Existence of the Triune God, who as uncreated Order and Rationality is the Source, Author and Fulfiller of all.

I let Gregory, therefore, have the last word from Oration XLV: the Second Oration on Easter:XXIX-XXX, written and delivered in celebration of *the rising of the Great Light* (II).

> Many indeed are the miracles of that time: God crucified; the sun darkened and again rekindled; for it was fitting that creatures should suffer with their Creator; the veil rent; the Blood and Water shed from His Side; the one as from a man, the other as above man; the rocks rent for the Rock's sake; the dead raised for a pledge of the final Resurrection of all men; the Signs at the Sepulchre and after the Sepulchre, which none can worthily celebrate; and yet none of these are equal to the Miracle of my salvation. A few drops of Blood recreate the whole world, and become to all men what rennet is to milk, drawing us together and compressing us into unity.
>
> But, O Pascha, great and holy and purifier of all the world – for I will speak to thee as a living person – O Word of God and Light and Life and Wisdom and Might – for I rejoice in all Thy names – O Offspring and Expression and Signet of the Great Mind; O Word conceived and Man contemplated; Who bearest all things, binding them by the Word of Thy Power; receive this discourse ...

Epilogue

THE INTRIGUING marvel of physical light, its elusiveness, its ubiquity, its precise action and effect, and the wonder of mental enlightenment as a particular process within and related to this whole phenomenon of *lux benigna*, that good and beneficial light, allow it a paradeigmatic priority in assisting faith seeking understanding. Above all, these qualities of created light bestow upon it an aura of mystery, which excites the mind to turn to the greater mystery of the beginning, sustaining and purpose of all existence to which the enigma of light points as that to which it is inseparably related. There is, as it were, a natural bond, intuitively perceived by the human mind because of the constant and determinative action of light at all levels of created existence, between created light and uncreated Light.

However, we have heard already Grosseteste's cautionary advice (pp. 58–59) to be aware of the danger of projecting unperceived creaturely unsuitabilities in the more immaterial existences, light above all, when applying them as illustrations to assist the mind towards the knowledge of God. And we have heard already also Gregory Nazianzen's reluctance in the matter (pp. 146–147). There should always be a constant awareness of the qualitative distinction between that which is created and the uncreated Existence of God, and therefore of the inappropriate nature of any created thing, however 'pure', as that which may be applied directly to that which is uncreated.

It is only at the incarnation, as the union of uncreated Light and created Light, of these as Word and human creature, that symbols find what paradeigmatic propriety they have for this end. Lancelot Andrewes[1] uses the action of light as an illustration of the incarnation itself. In this usage, he distinguishes between 'light' and the 'maker of light', yet perceives the relation between them, and implicitly but clearly uses the natural mystery of light to point to the mystery of the 'how' of the incarnation. He does so by bringing in, as a sub-text, Acts XXVI:8.

> But I aske Saint Pauls question: *Why should it be thought a thing incredible, this* to the Gentiles; if, (as their Religion taught them) they admitted, of *Minerva's* birth, or *Pyrrha's* progeny, they need not make strange, at this. If they say, the GOD of Nature is not bound to the rules of Nature: we say the same. And yet, even in Nature, we see it made not altogether incredible. The light passing thorow a body, the body yet remaining whole: And it is put therefore into the Verse, to patterne this *Luce penetratur, etc.* The light commeth thorow the glasse, yet the glasse is not perished. No more, than the light of Heaven, passing thorow, breaketh the glasse; No more, did the GOD of Heaven, by His passage, violate any whit, the Virginity of His Mother; if we will allow GOD the maker of the light, to doe as much as the light, He hath made.

This 'allow God' is the essence of faith. We have looked at the relation between faith and understanding in the knowledge of God in terms of Anselm's dictum in the matter. Faith will always be one step ahead of the understanding we have from it as it moves on and penetrates more and more the mystery which God is. But faith will always allow the mystery of God to be just that; it will not seek to comprehend it by understanding, for, to paraphrase Athanasius's remark,[2] when we are dealing with the things of God, we are in the place where even the cherubim veil their faces and seraphim spread the covering of their wings. Thus also Hilary of Poitiers:[3]

> The perfect knowledge of God is so to know him that we are sure that we must not be ignorant of him, yet cannot describe him. We must believe, must apprehend, must worship; and such acts of devotion must stand in lieu of definition.

Likewise Basil the Great with his observation that God can only, in the last resort, be worshipped in silence. The constant awareness of so many of the fathers that in undertaking the pursuit of theology they were treading on holy ground prevented that impudent trespass into the mystery of God which characterizes some 'theologies' whose object of discussion is scarcely dissimilar to what humanity vaunts

333

itself to be according to its prevailing but evanescent vogue of self-induced vision. Such deities do not command the reverence of worship; rather they attract loud distractive and detached debate.

That light is inextricably bound to the Being of God, the Self-revelation of God, and the being of his creatures, is a safeguard against such straying into such labyrinthine speculation, if for no other reason than its inherent mystery commands respect towards it and the necessity of letting it come to us on its own terms. The full nature of created light, and the astounding way in which our understanding is linked to that nature, defies the shallow search and the facile answer.

Three of the figures to whom I have appealed largely in the midst of citing others – Gregory of Nazianzen from the fourth century, Anselm from the late 11th, early 12th centuries, and Robert Grosseteste from the thirteenth century, all are aware of the magnificence of light and the overwhelming way in which the mind is brought up short by what is suggested by light in opening up the pondering of the reality and character and purpose of all creation, and beyond that, to the mystery which the Creator is. How reverently they tread the path of tracing the relation between uncreated Light and this universe of light, and how humbly they recognize the place of the human mind in such a venture. If not only the fruits of their thinking, but the attitude of mind which they adopt in pursuit of truth, were to be an essential quality of all theological endeavour, so much of the all too common tragic superficiality and banal comment on God and the things of God might well be avoided, and the Self-revealing integrity of God and, in that light, the proper dignity of humanity and the profound rationality of all creation, more wonderingly and thankfully appreciated, grasped and valued.

In the three books which form this trilogy of Time, Space and Light, I have spoken of the three-dimensional absurdities into which just such superficial testament of God and humanity and creation can lead us. Time can be elevated from being merely a measurement of convenience into a supposed entity in itself – Space likewise. In both *The*

Anachronism of Time and *The Dynamism of Space*, I have argued that these supposed categories are but expressions of existence both individually and in their relation to other existences. As characteristics of existence, they have their source and their purpose and their direction and their fulfilment in God, the Author and Perfecter of all things. The relation of creation to the Creator is seen in that time and place which is the Person and event of the Word made flesh.

That is where an understanding of what is truly meant by 'time' and 'space', and the description of this universe as a 'temporal-spatial creation' becomes possible. For the incarnation is the context of the temporal-spatial realties in their relation to their Creator who is God in all his uncreated Rationality. It is there that the gulf appears between what we call 'eternity' and what we call 'time', between what we call 'finitude' and what we call 'infinity', between what we think of as 'heaven' and what we think we know of 'earth'. It is there that God makes 'time' and 'place' for us, but by becoming man, assuming our humanity to himself. Jesus Christ is the time and place of God for his creation, and in him the time and place of creation is lifted up into a community of union with the eternal time and infinite place of God – but only because there is a union of God and man. The reality of the Existence of God in all his Godness in the midst of the realities of the created order, taking these into union with himself, is what time and space are all about. In other words we cannot divorce time and space from concrete existence, and the existence of creation can only be understood in the light of its Creator.

Light itself that which is time and space, for, fundamentally, light is life and life is light. *With Thee is the well of life; and in Thy Light we see light*, is our watchword here with the Psalmist. Created light causes 'time' and 'space' because it causes existence. In Jesus Christ where the uncreated Light of God is brought to bear on the realities of this creation, created light is established and grounded in its Source, pointing all existence to its Source.

This Christocentric emphasis in the theological usage of light is strong throughout the writings of those theologians who, throughout the course of theology, have recognized the unique place of light in relation to matter and mind. It is here, in the Word made flesh, and in the subjection of all our presuppositions about 'time' and 'space' and light to his determining and controlling Truth as the Light of the World, Light of Light, Very God of Very God, that a unitary view of creation in its relation to the Creator, becomes possible.

I have pointed out already in the two earlier books, that what I have written is not be construed as conclusions on the matter. Rather, these books, and this third, are offered in the hope that they will encourage others to take up these related themes of time and space and light, and advance a theological understanding of them further than I am able. I trust that they will be read and understood in this light.

Created light itself, the nature of time and space, because it is existence, rationality and order, corresponding to the uncreated Light of God, can only point us ever and again to that God in a quest of faith seeking understanding. I let the worship of the fourth century Church have the final word:

> Hail, gladdening Light, of His pure glory pour'd
> Who is the immortal father, heavenly, blest
> Holiest of Holies, Jesus Christ our Lord!
> Now we are come to the sun's hour of rest,
> The lights of evening round us shine;
> We hymn the Father, Son, and Holy Spirit Divine.
> Worthiest art Thou at all times to be sung
> With undefiled tongue,
> Son of our God, Giver of life, alone;
> Therefore in all the world Thy glories, Lord, they own.
>
> (4th Century: tr. John Keble).

Notes

Prologue
1. I Timothy VI:16.
2. Grosseteste: *De Luce.*

Chapter One: Light: the first of all creation
1. Basil: Hexaemeron I:3.
2. (Ed.) J. B. Pritchard: Ancient Near Eastern Texts relating to the Old Testament, pp. 60–72.
3. Karl Barth: Church Dogmatics III:1 pp. 102ff.
4. Karl Barth: Church Dogmatics III:1 pp. 108ff.
5. Augustine: Confessions XII:13ff.
6. Augustine: Confessions XII:13.
7. Swan, J: Speculum Mundi 1643 edition, pp. 42f.
8. Basil: Hexaemeron II:1ff.
9. Basil: Hexaemeron III:3.
10. Basil: Hexaemeron: I:6.
11. Pseudo-Dionysius: The Celestial Hierarchy 165A; c.f. 180B.
12. Pseudo-Dionysius: The Celestial Hierarchy 177Cff; c.f. The Divine Names 693Bff.
13. Pseudo-Dionysius: The Celestial Hierarchy 181Bff.
14. Pseudo-Dionysius: The Celestial Hierarchy 208C.
15. Pseudo-Dionysius: The Divine Names 693Bff.

Chapter Three: Light: the first of all forms; Comment on Grosseteste's *De Luce*.
1. McEvoy, J: The Philosophy of Robert Grosseteste (Clarendon, 1986), pp. 516ff.
2. Southern, R: Robert Grosseteste: The Growth of an English Mind in Medieval Europe (Clarendon, 1988), p. 136.
3. Southern, R: Robert Grosseteste: The Growth of an English Mind in Medieval Europe, p. 138.
4. Grosseteste, R: Hexaemeron II:X:4 (Dales and Gieben, Oxford for the British Academy, 1982: p. 100).
5. Commentaries in VIII Libros Physicorum Aristotelis.
6. Commentaries in VIII Libros Physicorum Aristotelis.
7. Basil: Hexaemeron: II:7.
8. Grosseteste, R: Hexaemeron: II:X:4 (Dales and Gieben, p. 100).

Chapter Four: The Constancy of Created Light and the Nature of God
1. Dales, R: art. in Viator 2, 1971.
2. Dales, R: art. in Viator 9, 1978, p. 179.
3. Pseudo-Dionysius: The Divine Names: 697C–701B.
4. Psuedo-Dionysius: The Divine Names: 700B.
5. Pseudo-Dionysius: The Divine Names: 701C.
6. Pseudo-Dionysius: The Divine Names: 701D.
7. Pseudo-Dionysius: The Divine Names: 704B.

Chapter Five: The Unity and Diversity of Created Light and the Nature of God
1. Psalm XXXVI:9.
2. Pseudo-Dionysius: The Divine Name: 697B–701B.
3. Grosseteste, R: Hexaemeron II:X:4 (Dales and Gieben, p. 100).
4. Grosseteste, R: Hexaemeron: VIII:IV:7 (Dales and Gieben, p. 222).
5. Torrance, T. F: Christian Theology and Scientific Culture, pp. 103ff (Christian Journals Limited, Belfast, 1980).
6. McEvoy, J: The Philosophy of Robert Grosseteste: p. 321.
7. Southern, R: Robert Grosseteste: The Growth of an English Mind in Medieval Europe, pp. 217–218.
8. Einstein, A: Out of My Later Years, p. 33 (The Philosophical Library, New York, 1950).
9. Einstein, A: The World as I See It, p. 18 (J. Lane, 1935).

Chapter Six: Light, Words and the Word of God
1. Torrance, T. F: e.g. Christian Theology and Scientific Culture: pp. 109ff.
2. C.f. Gregory Nazianzen: Fifth Oration: On the Holy Spirit XXI; Irenaeus: Adversus Haereses IV:XXVI:1.
3. Irenaeus: Adversus Haereses IV:XX:7.
4. Irenaeus: Adversus Haereses II:XIII:8; c.f. II:XXVIII:4–6.
5. Ambrose: On the Christian Faith I:58:74.
6. Gregory Nazianzen: Oration XXVIII, the Second Theological Oration, IX; c.f. Athanasius: Ad Mon. 2; Basil: Con Eun. I:10.

Chapter Seven: Light, Words, Understanding and the Knowledge of God
1. Anselm: Proslogion 1–157.
2. Anselm: Proslogion 47–51.
3. Anselm: Proslogion 72–74.
4. Anselm: Proslogion 80.
5. Anselm: Proslogion 75–142.

6. Anselm: Proslogion 154–157.
7. Anselm: Proslogion Preface.
8. Anselm: Proslogion Preface.
9. Anselm: Proslogion 161.
10. Anselm: Proslogion 159–160.
11. Anselm: Proslogion 518–519.
12. Anselm: Proslogion 659–674.
13. Anselm: Proslogion 656–658.
14. Torrance, T. F: Reality and Evangelical Theology, (The Westminster Press, Philadelphia, 1982) pp. 127ff.

Chapter Eight: The 'Obscurism' of Light and the Nature of God
1. Andrewes, L: Sermon III Of the Nativitie: XCVI Sermons, 1635 ed., pp. 17ff.
2. Davies, P. and Gribbin, J: The Matter Myth (Penguin Books, 1992) p. 20.
3. Anselm: Meditation on Human Redemption 129–131.
4. Anselm: Meditation on Human Redemption 188ff.
5. Torrance, T. F: Christian Theology and Scientific Culture, pp. 92f.
6. Basil: De Spiritu Sancto 47.

Chapter Nine: Light, the Word, the Spirit and Humanity
1. Athanasius: Ad Serapionem I:27.
2. Gregory Nazianzen: The Fifth Theological Oration: On the Holy Spirit III.
3. Gregory Nazianzen: The Fifth Theological Oration: On the Holy Spirit VIII.
4. Gregory Nazianzen: Oration XLI On Pentecost IX.
5. Gregory Nazianzen: The Fifth Theological Oration: On the Holy Spirit XXXII–XXXIII.
6. Gregory Nazianzen: The Fifth Theological Oration: On the Holy Spirit XXVI.
7. Basil: De Spiritu Sancto 22.
8. Torrance, T. F: The Trinitarian Faith (T. and T. Clark, 1988), p. 214.
9. Athanasius: Ad Serapionem I:14.
10. Irenaeus: Adversus Haereses IV:XIV:1.
11. Irenaeus: Adversus Haereses IV:VI:4.
12. Irenaeus: Adversus Haereses II:XIX:2.
13. Irenaeus: Adversus Haereses V:XIV:1,2; c.f. III:XXIII:1, 2.
14. Irenaeus: Demonstration of the Apostolic Preaching 2.
15. Irenaeus: Demonstration of the Apostolic Preaching 7; c.f. 3.
16. Irenaeus: Demonstration of the Apostolic Preaching 3.
17. Irenaeus: Adversus Haereses IV:XX:7.

18. Athanasius: Contra Arianos III:52.
19. Athanasius: Contra Arianos III:53.
20. Calvin J: Institutio I:1:2.
21. II Corinthians IV:6.

Chapter Ten: Light, the Trinity, Baptism and the Christian Life

1. Gregory Nazianzen: Oration XXXIX: On the Holy Lights I.
2. Gregory Nazianzen: Oration XXXIX: On the Holy Lights II.
3. Gregory Nazianzen: The Fifth Theological Oration: On the Holy Spirit III.
4. Gregory Nazianzen: Oration XLII: The Last Farewell XV.
5. Gregory Nazianzen: Oration XXIX: On the Son XVI.
6. Gregory Nazianzen: Oration XL: On Holy Baptism XLI.
7. Gregory Nazianzen: c.f., for example, Oration II: In Defence of His Flight to Pontus 37; Oration XVII: On the Death of His Father 16; Oration XXI: On the Great Athanasius 13, 34; the Fifth Theological Oration: On the Holy Spirit XVI; Oration XXXIV: On the Arrival of the Egyptians VIII; implied in Oration XXXVIII: On the Theophany XV; Oration XLII: The Last Farewell 16, etc.
8. Gregory Nazianzen: Oration XXXIX: On the Holy Lights XI.
9. Gregory Nazianzen: Oration XXI: On the Great Athanasius 35.
10. Gregory Nazianzen: Oration XXI: On the Great Athanasius 31.
11. Gregory Nazianzen: The Fifth Theological Oration: On the Holy Spirit XXXI, XXXII.
12. Gregory Nazianzen: Oration XXXIX: On the Holy Lights XI.
13. Gregory Nazianzen: Oration XL: On Holy Baptism V.
14. Gregory Nazianzen: Oration XL: On Holy Baptism V.
15. Gregory Nazianzen: Oration XL: On Holy Baptism V.
16. Gregory Nazianzen: Oration XL: On Holy Baptism V.
17. Gregory Nazianzen: c.f. Oration XL: On Holy Baptism VII.
18. Gregory Nazianzen: Oration XL: On Holy Baptism V.
19. Gregory Nazianzen: Oration XLV: the Second Oration on Easter IV.
20. Gregory Nazianzen: Oration XLV: the Second Oration on Easter V.
21. Gregory Nazianzen: Oration XLV: the Second Oration on Easter VI.
22. Gregory Nazianzen: Oration XLV: the Second Oration on Easter VI.
23. Gregory Nazianzen: Oration XLV: the Second Oration on Easter VII.

24. Gregory Nazianzen: Oration XLV: the Second Oration on Easter VII.
25. Gregory Nazianzen: Oration XL: On Holy Baptism VI.
26. Gregory Nazianzen: Oration XLV: the Second Oration on Easter VIII (copied in Oration XXXVIII: On the Theophany XII)
27. Irenaeus: Demonstration of the Apostolic Preaching 12; c.f., for example, Adversus Haereses IV: XXXVIII:1, 2.
28. Irenaeus: Demonstration of the Apostolic Preaching 15.
29. Gregory Nazianzen: Oration XXXIX: On the Holy Lights VII.
30. Gregory Nazianzen: Oration XXXIX: On the Holy Lights VIII.
31. Gregory Nazianzen: Oration XL: On Holy Baptism X.
32. Gregory Nazianzen: Oration XL: On Holy Baptism XVI.
33. Gregory Nazianzen: Oration XL: On Holy Baptism XVII.
34. Gregory Nazianzen: Oration XL: On Holy Baptism XVIII.
35. Gregory Nazianzen: Oration XL: On Holy Baptism XIII.
36. Irenaeus: Adversus Haereses II:XXII:4.
37. Irenaeus: Adversus Haereses III:XVIII:7.
38. Gregory Nazianzen: Oration XL: On Holy Baptism XIII.
39. Gregory Nazianzen: Oration XXXVIII: On The Theophany XVIII.
40. Gregory Nazianzen: Oration XXXIX: On the Holy Nights XX.
41. Gregory Nazianzen: Oration XXXIX: On the Holy Lights XIII.
42. Gregory Nazianzen: Oration XL: On Holy Baptism III–IV.
43. Gregory Nazianzen: Oration XL: On Holy Baptism VI.
44. Gregory Nazianzen: Oration XL: On Holy Baptism X.
45. Gregory Nazianzen: Oration XXXVIII: On the Theophany XIII.
46. The Fifth Theological Oration: On the Holy Spirit XXVI–XXVII.
47. Gregory Nazianzen: c.f., for example, Oration XII: To His Father 4; Oration XXXIX: On the Holy Lights IX, XI; Oration XLV: the Second Oration on Easter III; Epistle CI: To Cledonius).
48. Gregory Nazianzen: Oration XLV: the Second Oration on Easter III.
49. Gregory Nazianzen: Oration XL: On Holy Baptism XXXVI – citing Isaiah L:11.
50. Gregory Nazianzen: c.f. for example, Oration XL: On Holy Baptism V–VI.
51. Gregory Nazianzen: Oration XL: On Holy Baptism XXXVII.
52. Gregory Nazianzen: Oration XL: On Holy Baptism XXXVIII.

53. Gregory Nazianzen: Oration XL: On Holy Baptism XXXIX–XLI.

Epilogue
1. Andrewes, L: Sermon 9 on the Nativitie, 1635 edition p. 74.
2. Athanasius: Ad Serapionem: I:17; In Illud Omnia: 6.
3. Hilary of Poitiers: De Trinitate: II:7; c.f. II:6, 11; III:1–5; IV:1ff; XI:41–44.

Select Bibliography

Andrewes, Lancelot: *XCVI Sermons*, 1635 edition.

Anselm: *Opera*; Migne.

Athanasius: *Select Works, A Select Library of Nicene and Post-Nicene Fathers*, 1891.

Augustine: *Select Works, A Select Library of Nicene and Post-Nicene Fathers*, 1886.

Barth, Karl: *Church Dogmatics*, vols.I:1 and 2; II:1, 2; III:1, 2, 3 and 4; IV:1, 2, 3: T. and T. Clark, 1956–1975.

Basil: *Select Works, A Select Library of Nicene and Post-Nicene Fathers*, 1894.

Calvin, John: *Institutes of the Christian Religion*, trans. H. Beveridge, Eerdmans, 1979.

Davies, P. and Gribbin, J: *The Matter Myth*, Penguin Books, 1992.

Einstein, Albert: *Out of My Later Years*, The Philosophical Library, New York, 1950; *The World as I See It*, J. Lane, 1935.

Gregory Nazianzen: *Select Works, A Select Library of Nicene and Post-Nicene Fathers*, 1893.

Gregory of Nyssa: *Select Works, A Select Library of Nicene and Post-Nicene Fathers*, 1892.

Grosseteste, Robert: *De Cessatione Legalium*; *Hexaemeron*, texts by Dales and Gieben, Oxford University Press for the British Academy; *Commentaries on VIII Libros Physicorum Aristotelis*; *De Luce*.

Hilary of Poitiers: *Select Works, A Select Libary of Nicene and Post-Nicene Fathers*, 1898.

Irenaeus: *Select Works, The Ante-Nicene Fathers, Edinburgh Edition*, 1884; *Demonstration of the Apostolic Preaching*, trans. J. Armitage Robinson, S.C.M. 1935.

McEvoy, James: *The Philosophy of Robert Grosseteste*, Clarendon Press, Oxford, 1986.

MacKenzie, Iain: *The Anachronism of Time*, The Canterbury Press Norwich, 1994; *The Dynamism of Space*, The Canterbury Press Norwich, 1995.

Origen: *Select Works, The Ante-Nicene Fathers, Edinburgh Edition*, 1885.

Pseudo-Dionysius: *Works*, Migne, 1857.

Southern, Richard: *Robert Grosseteste, The Growth of an English*

Mind in Medieval Europe, Clarendon Press, Oxford, 1988.

Swan, John: *Speculum Mundi or a Glasse Representing the Face of the World*, 1643 Edition.

Torrance, Thomas: *Christian Theology and Scientific Culture*, Christian Journals, Belfast, 1980; *The Ground and Grammar of Theology*, Christian Journals, Belfast, 1980; *Theology in Reconciliation*, Geoffrey Chapman, 1975; *Theology in Reconstruction*, SCM Press, 1965; *God and Rationality*, Oxford University Press, 1971; *Space, Time and Incarnation*, Oxford University Press, 1969; *Space, Time and Resurrection*, The Handsel Press, 1976; *Theological Science*, Oxford University Press, 1978; *Transformation and Convergence in the Frame of Knowledge*, Christian Journals, Belfast, 1984; *Divine and Contingent Order*, Oxford University Press, 1981; *The Trinitarian Faith*, T. and T. Clark, 1988.

Index